The
Care & Feeding
of Volunteers

Creative Leadership Series

Assimilating New Members, Lyle E. Schaller
Beginning a New Pastorate, Robert G. Kemper
The Care and Feeding of Volunteers, Douglas W. Johnson
Creative Stewardship, Richard B. Cunningham
Time Management, Speed B. Leas
Your Church Can Be Healthy, C. Peter Wagner
Leading Churches Through Change, Douglas Alan Walrath
Building an Effective Youth Ministry, Glenn E. Ludwig
Preaching and Worship in the Small Church,
William Willimon and Robert L. Wilson
Church Growth, Donald McGavran and George G. Hunter III
The Pastor's Wife Today, Donna Sinclair
The Small Town Church, Peter J. Surrey
Strengthening the Adult Sunday School Class, Dick Murray
Church Advertising, Steve Dunkin
Women as Pastors, edited by Lyle E. Schaller
Leadership and Conflict, Speed B. Leas
Church Finance in a Complex Economy, Manfred Holck, Jr.
The Tithe, Douglas W. Johnson
Surviving Difficult Church Members, Robert D. Dale
Your Church Has Personality, Kent R. Hunter
The Word on Families, G. William Sheek

The
Care & Feeding
of Volunteers

Douglas W. Johnson

Creative Leadership Series
Lyle E. Schaller, Editor

Abingdon Press / Nashville

CARE AND FEEDING OF VOLUNTEERS

Library of Congress Cataloging in Publication Data

JOHNSON, DOUGLAS W., 1934-
    Care and feeding of volunteers.
    (Creative leadership series)
    1. Church work. I. Title. II. Series.
    BV4400.J53   254'.6   78-8295

ISBN 0-687-04669-6

MANUFACTURED BY THE PARTHENON PRESS AT
NASHVILLE, TENNESSEE, UNITED STATES OF AMERICA

George Watt, Jr.

and the staff of

Ridgewood United Methodist Church

Foreword

One of the most critical tests of creative leadership in the church is the development and maintenance of a corps of volunteer workers and leaders. The worshiping congregation is a voluntary association, and in many respects, the typical congregation resembles such more than it does a called-out community of believers. This is one of the reasons many congregations often have difficulty finding enough volunteer workers. Too often the leaders assume that the religious commitment of the individual member is in itself a sufficient motivating force to produce the necessary volunteers, but that is a most fallacious assumption!

In this volume Doug Johnson offers a more realistic and effective approach to the development and maintenance of a cadre of volunteers. The first chapter identifies several of the distinctive characteristics of a typical volunteer. It suggests what a volunteer is not, and what makes a volunteer run.

A basic assumption that is of critical importance in maintaining a corps of individuals who willingly donate their spare time in any organization is that the volunteer is a human being and has real needs which merit serious attention. Dr. Johnson places a major emphasis throughout this entire volume on the agenda and concerns of such individuals as persons.

Dr. Johnson also demolishes the widely held assumption that there is a shortage of volunteers. Despite the rapid rise in the number of women employed outside the home, in the typical congregation between 30 and 65 percent of the members are willing to serve as workers and leaders in that congregation if they know they are needed, if they are challenged with a responsibility that matches their interests and abilities, if they are given meaningful assignments, and if they know their efforts are appreciated. (The smaller the congregation, the larger the proportion of the members willing to serve as volunteers.) This volume is filled with creative and practical suggestions on how to develop a larger staff of volunteers.

In an earlier volume in this series Robert Graham Kemper described the experience of moving into a new pastorate. To a limited degree this book can be seen as a companion volume to Kemper's. The newly arrived pastor could use the suggestions in this book as a checklist to evaluate the quality of the volunteer network in the new situation. After that evaluation has been completed, perhaps privately, the minister will find that this book offers many solid suggestions for improving the quality of the care and feeding of volunteers.

In other congregations one or two lay leaders have major responsibilities for identifying, recruiting, training, placing, and supporting that network of volunteers. For them this volume can be not only a guidebook on the "what" and "how" of carrying out their responsibilities, but also offers a realistic analysis of why certain steps are necessary in maintaining and expanding that network. The creative leader will find this an indispensible tool, not only in strengthening that network, but more important, in helping the contributions of the volunteer be a significant nurturing experience in the individual's own personal and spiritual growth.

Lyle E. Schaller
Yokefellow Institute

Preface

"If she would only let me alone, I could get this job done."

"We did our stint in the Sunday school when our kids were small. We are going to let some of the younger parents take over now. We want to be involved in the outreach of this congregation."

"I want to be involved in the work of the church but especially as it works in this community. I am very anxious for our church to be a moral force in this community."

"I'll do whatever needs to be done. My life has revolved around this church for years, and I want it to continue."

"I don't really think I can contribute much, but if you think I can be helpful, I will give it a try."

The voices of volunteers speak of motivations and frustrations, but the basic reason they work in the church is because it represents something that is meaningful and purposeful. It is a force for good in their lives and in the world. They feel that by working through it they may gain new learnings and new hope for their lives. They are self-giving but expect to receive something positive from their experience.

This spirit of giving time and effort is a key factor in the growth and vitality of the church. That the spirit is not diminished is indicated by a Gallup Poll in 1977, which showed 30 percent of the church members interviewed saying they worked as volunteers. The percentage was higher for persons fifty years of age and older and for those with college backgrounds. These statistics suggest that the age of volunteerism is yet to come as the population increases in the proportions of persons over fifty years and of those with college educations.

The test of an organization depending upon volunteers for its program is how well those persons do their jobs within the framework of the purposes of the organization. In the church this is called ministry and outreach. When a church encourages, trains, and supports volunteers to do a variety of jobs, it grows. When a congregation allows its pastor, church staff, or church leaders to limit the number of volunteers by discouraging them, by not allowing them to do their jobs, or by not providing training and support, that church stagnates and soon begins to decline. The attitude of church leaders can kill a congregation when that attitude stifles the initiative and creativity of the members who volunteer.

The issue of volunteers in the church is a vital one. The crux of the issue is not their availability. It is the manner in which they are recruited, trained, encouraged, supported, and allowed freedom to perform their jobs as ministry. In the church, the vitality of volunteers is directly controlled by the attitudes and feelings of the pastor and church leaders. This book deals with enabling volunteers in the church. Any criticism of pastors or church staff or church leaders in the book is based on the conviction that they have the power to release or inhibit volunteer energy in the church.

The discussion in the book, following the first chapter of a general overview and basic considerations in working with volunteers, deals with specific issues. The aim is to provide help for the pastors and church leaders who: identify and recruit, give assignments, help volunteers plan, run meetings, and train volunteers. My overriding concern is to utilize the desires, hopes, skills, and energies of people in the church so that witnessing communities may arise within congregations.

Contents

Chapter One: Volunteers in the Church 17
  Volunteers Are Important 18
  Volunteers Are Not Staff Members 20
  Simple Language 26
  Conserving Time and Energy 27
  Deadlines 29
  Work Quality 30
  Planning Style 31

Chapter Two: Identifying and Recruiting Volunteers 35
  Interest Approach 36
  Rest Periods 40
  Refusals 41
  Shy People 43
  Options 44
  Members Help Recruit 45
  Newcomer 48
  Recruitment Plan 50

Chapter Three: Giving Assignments 54
  Be Specific 57
  Don't Lie About Time 58
  What Is the Minister's Role? 61
  Fences and Boundaries 63

Work Plans 66
Time Tables and Check Backs 67
Providing Resources 70
Results 71

Chapter Four: Helping Volunteers Plan 74
A Planning Process 75
Start with a Plan 77
Interest Development 79
The Leader's Role 82
The "Big Picture" 84
Feedback 85
Summary 87

Chapter Five: Running Meetings 89
Purpose 91
Call to Meeting 92
Set the Time and Place 93
Meeting Time Plan 94
Adhere to the Schedule 97
Work the Agenda 100
Close on Time 101
Assignments 102
Minutes 106

Chapter Six: Training 108
Every Volunteer Needs Training 109
Customize the Training 112
Pictures and Experiences 117
Sequence of Job Steps 119
Resources 121
Flexibility 123
Conclusion 124

Chapter One
Volunteers in the Church

The woman hesitated slightly. Summoning her courage she walked into the office. The clergyman looked up, surprised. "Hello. What can I do for you?" He could not recall the woman's name although her face looked familiar.

"I am June May. This is Tina and this is Tom." She motioned to the two small children with her. "I was wondering about doing something for the church. I don't work, and I want to do something constructive. Is there anything I can do?"

The board meeting was continually bogging down. The leader was a nice person who was so busy in other activities that she did not have the time to plan. One evening a retired businessman called the pastor. "Do you mind," he asked, "if I spend some time with Mrs. Winrow to help her plan our board meetings? I think there are a couple of things I can advise her on that will speed up the meetings and yet get the work done. Anyway, I have some time this next month, and this might be the best way to spend it."

A minister received a call from a young man. "I was wondering, pastor, if you need any help with the youth group. I am interested and would like to help out for a few months, maybe even the whole year. Jenny, my steady girl friend, is willing to work with me. We would need some help from you in the programs and all, but we feel we can do this for the church."

These are three kinds of persons who want to do something worthwhile with their time and their lives. They have sought out the church. They are volunteers, the people who make possible the program and outreach of the church.

Volunteers come in various shapes and sizes. They come to the church as competent, good-hearted, trained, untrained, bright, not so bright, or even selfish, individuals. They are married, single, divorced, widowed. They are young, middle-aged, past middle age, or elderly. The list of attributes can be extended by each reader.

The physical characteristics and mental capabilities of volunteers are less critical than two other more important traits. First, volunteers give time and energy to the church. They are rewarded for their efforts in ways other than monetary. As such, they provide a valuable resource without reimbursement for time, talents, and energies.

Secondly, volunteers want to do something worthwhile for and through the church. Cynical observers have said that volunteers are people who give time to fulfill selfish needs, to accomodate guilt feelings and similar motivational factors. These observations may be applicable to some volunteers. These are not the feelings about volunteers on which this book is based. Instead, volunteers are viewed as persons who want to make a difference in their and other people's lives. They see the church as a means for making their contribution to others. A volunteer in the church wants to do something that provides depth and dimension to his or her life at the same time it expresses help to others.

Volunteers Are Important

These two characteristics of church volunteers are important for church leaders to recognize. Volunteers may be burdensome at times, but in the long run, their time and efforts make the church function. They are its corps of witnesses in the world.

At times their intentions may seem obscure to the pastor or church staff. For example, the pastor of a congregation receives a call from a woman who wants to give some time to the church. She thinks she can do office work, especially typing, since she worked in an office when she was younger. She has one condition. She cannot spend any time at the church office since she has four small children. Is there anything she can do at home to help out?

How does the pastor respond? Does he or she ask the woman why she wants to work in the church? Should he or she suggest that instead of doing typing she consider serving on a committee that meets one night a month? What is the approach of a pastor to such a request?

The pastor knows that this woman with experience and time available is important to any church. The church like most others has work that can be done by additional typists. Envelopes can be addressed, reports, sermons, and newsletters can be typed. All are jobs that can be farmed out to a typist at home. Unfortunately, the church has a limit to the number of typists it can use. In addition, there is the problem of typewriters, supplies, and the like. These issues can be worked out, but the pastor chooses to explore the alternative use of time with this woman. In so doing, he attempts to help this woman as a person search for a way she can express her ministry in the church.

An organization dependent on volunteers learns that it must encourage and motivate volunteers even though this takes much time and energy. Developing warm and good feelings among nonpaid workers is a continuing task. After all, volunteers are the most important resources a church can have in spite of the frustrations and problems they pose at times. On the other hand, ministers and church staff can be frustrating and create problems for volunteers.

The importance of volunteers in the church was underscored by a pastor in a large church in the Southwest. He was in a meeting that was running over time. He asked to be excused for a minute explaining that he had a call to make and an appointment within half an hour. The nature of these obligations suggested the need for him to take care of them rather than continue with the meeting. When the chairperson suggested that the meeting could be rescheduled, the pastor smiled and said, "No. Joe Skinner can handle both of these situations. He is a very competent lay volunteer who will take over for me. If he has a problem, he will let me know."

This pastor worked hard at recruiting and training lay persons. He and they believed that a congregation can function in most of its life without a clergy person. They were practicing the obvious. Most congregations can exist during a clergy person's vacation or times of illness or during the weeks or months between clergy persons. Churches do not close simply because a clergy person is not around. On the other hand, no church can exist for a month without volunteers. All of the committees, finances, and teaching duties are volunteer responsibilities. The volunteer is an essential and necessary part of the church. Without him or her, it cannot long exist.

Volunteers Are Not Staff Members

Volunteers must be regarded as volunteers. While this seems obvious, it is not. It is a concept that will require some adjustments in the thinking of some professional church leaders. They sometimes confuse a steady volunteer with a staff person. They may understand that volunteers are motivated in part by the attitude of the minister. They may not comprehend that time is a gift to the church and the cost for maintaining the volunteer's relationship is a certain amount of time and energy on their part. Ministers are key factors in getting and keeping volunteers. The ministers' understanding of their own role and the way they view volunteers is critical to the life of the church.

Volunteers do create problems and frustrations. They are persons and, as humans, they bring their prejudices, feelings, and excitement with them. Ministers, and staff members in larger churches, through their understanding of the nature of church work and a sympathetic attitude toward volunteers, can help them perform their tasks better. Preparation of both the volunteers and the minister can be quite helpful.

Volunteers are people in active ministry. A part of the ministry of a congregation is to provide the means whereby volunteers can express their witness and service in a fulfilling manner.

The concept of volunteerism as ministry is not new for some ministers. However, other ministers and church leaders have quite a different feeling about volunteers. For example, ministers in some churches review the qualifications of volunteers as though they are hiring an additional staff member. Still others treat volunteers as individuals with limited intelligence and unlimited time. Neither of these approaches does justice to either the volunteer or the church.

In some congregations the minister or a secretary or some other individual tries to do all the jobs without volunteers. The ego needs of such a person are so great that he or she cannot allow others to share the ministry. The inevitable result is that the church program is stifled, and others are not involved in the church's vitality. In time, the church has no life to speak of.

On the other hand, the churches that make the best use of their volunteers have a positive philosophy. They view a volunteer as a person who wants to work through the church. The minister is not upset nor defensive because of them. He or she feels that volunteers are interested in the church and are not out to make over the entire program. These ministers know that each volunteer will seek to make some changes. These suggestions will be evaluated not only by the minister but by others in the church. If they are acceptable, the changes will become practice.

1. A volunteer is not . . .

What is a volunteer? Simply put, such a person is an individual willing to assist in the work of the church for no cost to the church. This definition can be clarified by identifying what volunteers are *not.*

(1) *Volunteers are not members of the staff.* This is the basis for volunteerism. This means that authority over volunteers by ministers or other staff members is limited. Although it is limited, authority, carefully used, can be exercised over the work quality of volunteers. Persuasion is a key word describing work with volunteers.

(2) *Volunteers are not full-time workers.* They give time and energy as they are able. During some weeks or months the amount of time given may be substantial while at other times they can give little or no time. There is an ebb and flow to each volunteer's life and consequently to the amount of energy available to give to the church. In any case, their lives are not fully involved in the church.

(3) *Volunteers cannot be taken for granted.* Volunteers are the determiners of whether or not they are going to give time and effort. This fact affects the relationships and the status volunteers occupy in a church. Their ties are emotional. Emotion, especially negative feelings created by their experiences as volunteers, can send them away as quickly as it brings them in.

(4) *Volunteers are not paid.* It is for this reason that churches

22

recognize the limits of the resources volunteers can invest. It costs a volunteer each time he or she does something for the church. This may be to pay a person to care for a child or an adult at home, hosting a meeting, or driving an auto. It is this recognition of expenses that compels some churches to reimburse volunteers for their out-of-pocket costs. While some persons refuse to take such payments, others are happy to have help with these extra expenses. An arrangement for occasional reimbursement takes little time and has great rewards. It shows that the church cares about the volunteer.

As an example, an elderly volunteer comes to the church office each Monday morning to address envelopes. During much of the year she can walk the half mile from her home to the church. It is good for her. However, when it rains, snows, or is cold, she has to take a bus or a taxi or get a ride from someone. Expenses like this are reimbursed so that she can continue to give time. These are small expenses for the church, but it means the difference between her activity or loneliness. The church, by giving these dollars, allows her a more fulfilling ministry through the church.

(5) *Volunteers are not bound to a job in the church for long periods of time.* A volunteer's life situation changes regularly. This means that a volunteer may be able to work for a month only. There is no mandate for a person to give time indefinitely. As life changes, capacities for and interest in volunteer work may increase or decrease. The safest assumption of a church leader regarding a volunteer is that the time commitment is temporary.

These five "nots" are helpful as guidelines in developing good relations with volunteers. This is the case especially for those persons who are quite active in a church, the regulars. As regulars, they sometimes are taken for granted and regarded as staff members. As such, their work assignments are considered long term. This attitude is not conducive to helping volunteers express ministry. It cripples them and the church. The other extreme is difficult as well, treating volunteers as capable of doing limited tasks.

2. Volunteers need . . .

The smart church leader views volunteers as talented persons with an integrity in work-style that does not need continual supervision. These leaders are careful to ensure that volunteers in their churches are able to meet their needs by doing their tasks. Such needs are the same as all persons experience.

(1) *Volunteers need to hear thanks.* Thanks is such a small word it often gets overlooked. At other times, when it is said, it is done in a gross fashion. It must be said with grace and meaning.

Two kinds of thanks turn off volunteers. The first comes in a request letter to do a job as a sentence that says, "Thank you in advance." This kind of perfunctory thank-you may save time and energy, but it does not endear a minister to volunteers. If a volunteer gives time, it seems that the least a minister could do is to say thanks in a phone call or in a brief personal note. Time is as important to volunteers as it is to a minister. The volunteer has to make an effort to free the time to do the job. A minister can free the time needed to make a call or a note.

The second kind of thank you is the form letter to which a volunteer's name is attached. An absence of a personal effort, other than writing in a name, raises questions about the worth of the activity on the part of the volunteer.

Personal thank-yous may use precious time. Smart church leaders give that time because they know that the manner of the thank-you conveys attitudes that encourage or discourage future gifts of time to the church.

One congregation uses a certificate of service award along

with a personal note from the pastor as a means of thanks. This certificate is designed especially for the church. It contains the name of the individual, the date of the award, and the task or service the volunteer has done. The certificate is given annually to all the volunteers at a special service.

(2) *Volunteers need recognition.* Few volunteers want to remain anonymous in their work in the church. It is a pleasure and provides an incentive for them to feel that their effort produces a needed service. This pleasure increases significantly when they are told that others feel the effort is important to the life of a congregation.

Being recognized publicly is good for the volunteer. Recognition at an important gathering is especially helpful. Many people live out their lives without public thanks or recognition by groups that mean the most to them. When persons have given time and energy in the church, it is among peers and friends. These friends and peers ought to be present at times of recognition.

Too much public recognition may be embarrassing. Recognition and public thanks are most effective when done sensitively.

(3) *Volunteers need to be treated courteously.* Volunteers, like all church members, ought to be treated with deference. For example, it may seem to a minister or the church staff like a volunteer is a close friend, but the relation ought to be that of nonintimate friends. Each has a distinct role and social place.

In the rough and tumble of meeting deadlines, dealing with people in crises, and keeping the program intact, feelings can be hurt and needs slighted. These are expected, but an alert minster tries to be courteous to all volunteers at all times. Rough language, rigid requirements, and unbending deadlines are only now and then applicable to volunteers and then only in highly defined circumstances.

These three needs are highlighted because they can be overlooked in work with volunteers. Praise can be given grudgingly. This is as bad as no praise at all. Recognition can be a tag end of an event, and thus lose its meaning. Treatment can be less than kind because a minister does not like a volunteer or feels that this person's work is inferior or tangential to the purpose of the church. None of these attitudes help either the volunteer or the minister.

Simple Language

"A professional creates jargon to mystify the lay person." This is the feeling of a professional who consciously uses a great deal of jargon. It provides him with an aura of professionalism which he feels he needs.

Jargon, as such, is used as a substitute for long explanations or orientation in a particular field of endeavor. A doctor uses doctor talk with associates to save time and energy. An engineer uses technical shorthand expressions to communicate among associates. The appropriate use of jargon is within a professional framework.

A problem with verbal shorthand is that to the non-experts, jargon is meaningless. The shorthand easily communicates among the professionals but becomes a puzzle for laity. This may not be apparent to the professional because people nod agreement. The user ought not to be encouraged by those nods. Some are made because the listeners feel they must respond. The simplest response is to nod. The nod does not signal understanding or insight so much as it does hope—hope that the speaker will explain the technical words and phrases to the listener.

A volunteer does not need to be impressed. They have more immediate needs. They need to know how to do the job they volunteered to do. When a parent volunteers to work with youth, for example, he or she is not helped by an analysis of various approaches to youth programming. The parent wants to know what is being done in this church and wants a brief statement of why. That parent needs to know about the available resources and their content.

It is the same situation when a person agrees to work in the area of evangelism. The various technical methods are not really important. The person wants to become active by using a particular approach in this church.

Professional jargon turns people off or it inhibits them. It is tempting to the minister to want to display expertise. The volunteer, however, wants to contribute something. If the pastor or person with whom the volunteer will work is addicted to catchy language, the volunteer will get an initial impression that a contribution will not be possible.

A person who wants to work with volunteers practices the art of simple language. Instead of, "We use the _____ method," they say, "Our aim is to get people active in the church, even those who have not been active for a while." This does two things for the volunteer. It makes it unnecessary to ask about a particular approach suggested by a minister. This, in turn, relieves any embarrassment because of a lack of knowledge about a particular philosophy and methodology. Secondly, it invites the volunteer to participate immediately in designing a process and identifying a target audience. It is action oriented.

In addition, simple language has the capacity of encouraging "aha" experiences. Technical language may give the impression that a novice's ideas are not imaginative nor creative enough for use in the church. It may suggest that new ideas or approaches are unwelcome. These outcomes or feelings are not the intent of a minister. Communication is best with simple, nontechnical language.

Conserving Time and Energy

Volunteers have a limited amount of time and energy to give. While some appear to have an inexhaustible supply of free time, this is not the case. Each volunteer must work out a personal schedule in order to free the time and make the energy available to the church.

An elderly lady wanted to give some time to the church. She was retired, had no relatives in the area, and was interested in doing as much as she could. "It gives me something to do," she told the pastor.

The pastor did not take her literally. He was a wise man. This woman belonged to several friendship clubs. Each had a regular meeting time. It was not that she was bound to attend each of the sessions, because they were all friendly get-togethers. Yet her attendance was important to her well-being. These sessions provided a peer group and a balance to the rhythm of her life.

The pastor did not know about these clubs. In fact, she never spoke of them except as she referred to one or another of her friends in conversation. He had established a rule about volunteers. "Do not take time from a person just because they say it is available."

This pastor used a "one person, one job" philosophy. Since this was the way he treated each volunteer, no one expected to do more. When people wanted to give more time, he encouraged them to become a volunteer in another organization. It helped keep them interesting and growing. It also helped keep them from feeling a proprietary relationship with the church.

This particular pastor practiced another strategy. He made certain, as much as was feasible, that a volunteer would not make unnecessary trips to see him. He took, or had taken, work to several volunteers. This was especially helpful in the case of elderly persons. He had discovered this practice to be critical for mothers with young children at home. Mothers often feel like taxi drivers, and for their volunteering to add more trips per week was enough to cut into their interest and enthusiasm.

Deadlines

Jobs have deadlines, and intentions to meet the schedule are a part of every volunteer's initial expectations. The reality of illness, claims on time from family and friends, and procrastination cut into everyone's ability to meet deadlines.

This does not mean that volunteers should have elastic deadlines or be given jobs where deadlines are not important. When a person takes a responsibility, it must be clear that the work must be done by such and such a time. "Tuesday at 8:00 P.M. we need your report," is the kind of deadline that people understand. They know what it means. Such clarity helps them plan in order to meet the schedule.

When a deadline is set, it ought to be realistic. Once set, it must not be ignored except in a clearly defined crisis. On the other hand, the deadlines must be established for a reason. If a person is told that a report is due for committee action, it behooves the minister to schedule action or hearings on it for that time. A deadline tests the credibility and trust of the minister just as much as it does the willingness of the volunteer to do a job.

One day a denominational executive called to ask a person to speak to a session of the Conference. They agreed on the time. Such an agreement usually requires a good bit of preparation and rearrangement of the personal activities of a speaker. When the day arrived, he got to the airport on time but spent an hour waiting for the executive to pick him up as promised. As last he called the Conference office.

"Hello. I am Ben Jones, the speaker for the evening session. I believe Dr. Bellow was to meet me at the airport at 10 o'clock. Is he on his way?"

"Oh. I'm so sorry, Mr. Jones. I will get the message to him right away. He will be right out."

Half an hour later Mr. Jones was greeted by a man who

introduced himself as Dr. Bellow's associate. "I am sorry to be so late. Our wires must have gotten crossed up. By the way, since we made our contact with you, the schedule has been rearranged. You will not speak at seven as originally planned, but at nine o'clock after another speaker."

This is gross unconcern for other people's feelings and time. While such events are not ordinary, too often there is laxity in engaging volunteers. A deadline to a minister is just an item on a daily or weekly calendar. This same item to a volunteer may be one entry also in a busy calendar, but it is a commitment that must be met. This may not be universal among volunteers, but the minister should feel such an attitude is normal. This perception on his or her part increases the possibility of maintaining the time integrity of both minister and volunteer. It exhibits a sensitivity to the claims of time on both.

Work Quality

In addition to keeping deadlines as firm as possible, the work quality of volunteers should be kept high. In a church in Illinois, there is a Christian education director whose life is a series of revised deadlines. An efficiency expert, looking at her work schedule would be appalled. This woman does not intend for her image to be thus, it is her style of work. She has a tendency to stretch deadlines. Some people feel that at the Second Coming, she will be unavailable because she will have rescheduled it.

What kind of work does she get from her volunteers? Excellent quality. Surprising? To some perhaps. She is a model in working with volunteers. She chooses the jobs carefully for each of her workers. That is one of the reasons she is behind schedule. She gives them a task only after she and they are quite clear on the type and quality of work that is expected. This usually takes more time than she allows originally. Deadlines are her only problem. She insists on quality by emphasizing that sloppy work is poor steward-ship of her time and of their energy.

She is an asset to the church primarily because she has an ability to select and train volunteers who do excellent work. One of her strengths as a leader is the number and quality of persons who help her get work done. Her example is important for those working with volunteers. Choose jobs to fit volunteers; be careful in instructions; establish specific deadlines; and insist upon quality work.

Planning Style

Volunteers want to help in the church. Most of them need assistance in planning what and how they are going to do their task. Every job has its special requirements. Volunteers do not know, usually, what these are unless they are told or find out the hard way. It saves much time and energy to work with people before they start a job. Effort at the beginning will save time by helping to avoid a botched up job later. It also eliminates a great deal of frustration on the part of both the minister and the volunteer.

In the same way that simple language is better than technical shorthand, simple planning is better than using complicated methods. The volunteer does not need a lesson in the principles of planning in order to get ready to do a job. Most important are instructions such as: "If you get this part of the job done by Wednesday and that part by next Monday, you will be ready to complete it by next Friday. To do this by Wednesday, you must call Jones, Gunther, and Domin. By next Monday, you will need, in addition to the calls, to fill out a form like this. The instructions are on the back of the page. Let's go through them now. By next Friday, you will need no more than one typewritten page, single-spaced with double spaces between paragraphs to present to the committee that evening. If it is done by 3:30 P.M., I will get it duplicated."

31

The instructions are simple and straightforward. This is the type of planning that is most helpful. It spreads the volunteer's work load and time commitment over two weeks. It identifies persons who must be contacted. The final report, based on a form with clear instructions, is one page long that will be considered by a committee. There is a possibility that the task could be completed in less time, and might be, depending on the work habits of the volunteer.

The critical elements are the instructions. These include a time schedule which identifies persons who will need to be contacted. There are landmarks on the way to the end of the job. Deadlines are included as a means of assisting the person in measuring progress. Included also is the element of reward. If the person gets the one page report in by a particular time, duplication will be cared for. Another form of reward is the consideration of the report by a committee.

The job assumes other things. It assumes actual dissemination of the work and a careful deliberation of its contents. This latter is a minister's responsibility. He or she must follow through to make it a fact. If a person works on a report for consideration at a particular meeting, the report ought to be reviewed then. If the volunteer does not meet the deadline, it is clear that his or her failure to carry out the assignment will have a detrimental effect on the committee. This assumption must be correct, or it cannot be a motivational force to the volunteer.

The process of planning should be direct. It will be participatory in that the volunteer may or may not adhere to the outline or schedule. The worst thing that can happen is for the job not to get done. Over this, the minister and volunteer have some control. The minister can assist the volunteer in doing a good job if a plan is agreed on which has checkpoints for completion of discrete elements of the task. People need specifics in timing and tasks. When these are not provided, minister and volunteers err.

Communicating with volunteers is being direct, appreciative, and simple. It is not assuming expertise or planning skills. These are bonuses that will be uncovered in time. At the outset: describe the task in simple terms; do not be condescending; be human; expect good work; look at the volunteer as an asset. The volunteer, on the other hand, should: ask questions when something is not clear; regard the minister or church staff as persons who can help; regard the job as a responsible trust; and let the minister know at the beginning if there are difficulties with the time schedule or work that will make the deadline hard or impossible to meet.

Volunteers are willing to do all manner of jobs including drudgery things for the church. However, they should not be expected to do any task the minister or church staff is unwilling to do. For example, in a small country church, it was necessary to get the fire started in the stove that heated the sanctuary each time there was a service.

An old man took it upon himself to do this job. It was his. He had to come an hour ahead of service time to start the kindling and get the fire going. Over time such a job becomes drudgery. It is not easy. No one really cares except when the church is cold. It behooves the minister in such situations to take a turn and relieve the man. Even if the man will not allow the minister to actually start the fire, being present, carrying the coal, or helping get the kindling ready shows concern and partnership. Some of my best moments in that little church were in the early Sunday morning talks with that man as he started the fire. He gave me more insights into the church and its members than I was able to get in a week of visiting.

There is nothing magical in working with volunteers. It is hard work, time-consuming, frustrating, and exciting. Volunteers will discover that these will be the same feelings they experience as they attempt to work through the church. In spite of these problems, the partnership of clergy and laity in tasks too great for either is the key to ministry through the church.

The following chapters provide some insights from experiences in churches that may assist in nurturing and guiding that privileged relationship between people in the church.

Chapter Two
Identifying and Recruiting Volunteers

The nominating committee is in an extra long session. The membership book is on the table. People around the table are tired. In front of each person is a sheet of paper with a list of names on it. One man wearily smiles and says, "There oughta be a better way. Recruitment shouldn't be this hard."

The pastor of a large congregation in the eastern part of the nation says, "If there is anything that would ever cause me to leave the ministry, it is recruiting volunteers. I hate to ask people to do this and that throughout the years. It puts me in the position of always begging."

A pastor in the Southwest says, "Our church is moving toward a totally volunteer staff. During the past two years, we have recruited volunteers to do all of the office work, to do visiting on a regular basis, and now we are working on developing a music program of volunteers. This is not an easy task since our church has 1,800 members."

The question these experiences pose for leaders is, "How can we find the right people to do a task?" There are corollary questions such as, "When does a person feel an overload?" "How can we help them say no?" "How can I discourage someone?" The issue is recruitment, that process by which people get interested, become volunteers, and get on with the job.

The tasks of identifying and recruiting volunteers is a mammoth and continuing one in every church. It is never finished although there are periods when there is less need for recruitment than at others. To recruit is to have volunteers. To be weary of the task of recruiting is to be human.

The most obvious approaches may not be the best. The ideas that comprise this chapter can assist church leaders in finding and putting volunteers to work. The stress is upon being innovative as well as practical.

Interest Approach

"She's a school teacher; let's ask her to be a teacher in the church school." "He works at the bank; let's see if he would be interested in being a member of the finance committee." "He is a builder; he can certainly help on the building committee." These statements are assumptions based on information about occupation. They are followed often in the recruitment processes.

This common assumption that persons who make their livelihood in certain professions are willing to use their expertise in a volunteer manner for the church are not supported by fact in many instances. Several persons accept occupation-oriented, volunteer work because they feel they should. Others do not do any volunteer work because they are not willing to be limited by their profession. Persons are in occupations due to early life choices. During the intervening years, interests have developed and hobbies have expanded that are more fulfilling than the occupation. The person has grown in ways other than their life's work. These ways are keys to happiness and fulfillment for the person now.

Recruiting volunteers on the basis of how they are

employed has a logic to it that is hard to overcome. Pastors are taught to ask people to do jobs that are somehow related to their jobs. Having applied this sage advice offered by seminary professors, experience raises the question as to why volunteers seem to be lackluster in their performance in occupation-related church jobs. A diminuitive school teacher provides a corrective to the professors.

"The last thing I want to do on Sunday morning is teach a group of kids. I do it all week long and need a rest—for my sake and theirs. Besides, I am a teacher of subjects other than those they learn on Sunday. I don't know any more about them than other people in the church. I will help in developing training for teachers and will serve on an education committee that sets policy for the total program, but I will not teach."

Strong words? Yes, for the pastor who asked her to teach. Lack of commitment? Not really. A negative response does not mean no commitment to the church. It reflects personal desires and needs at a particular time. In no way does it mean no commitment.

The issue raised by the teacher is important. Why should volunteers be put into vocational boxes? If volunteer work is an opportunity to express ministry through the church, the act of volunteering ought to be a form of continuing education and personal development for adults. It will mean training, learning, and new experiences. When this concept of volunteerism is used, it means that recruitment should not be automatically based on a person's occupation.

Volunteers must receive rewards other than money for their efforts. They do not expect money, but they desire growth and a sense of worth. A significant reward for many is a chance to be different and do things other than they are required to do as they earn their living or engage in their daily tasks. This is an idea that works.

For example, a mother with young children should not be

automatically thought to be interested in involvement in nursery care at the church. The young mother needs to do something unrelated to young children in order to grow herself. The church ought not restrict, but it should aid growth of volunteers.

This concept works as a two-edged sword. The recruiter must know more than a few cursory items about potential volunteers. If this is not true, he or she must be willing to encourage volunteers to participate in the church by providing a variety of options from among which to choose.

This process of interest recruitment requires more knowledge by the leadership of the people in the congregation than is normally the case. When interest is the key rather than vocation, some deeper insights into people's lives are essential. This does not rule out the possibility that interest and occupation might be the same for some persons.

Not all persons are able to function successfully along interest rather than vocational lines. Such individuals may be afraid of failure, feel insecure in a new field, or do not want to expose their reputation or status on something like an interest. Such individuals can be convinced to change if the interest is strong. Usually a change requires the recruiter to give a lot of time in resourcing and providing emotional support. It is within reason to consider this support through personal contact as a part of pastoral ministry. One or two successful ventures are enough usually to enable reluctant individuals to be more willing to do new things in the future.

How can we identify interests? We may not have the time to have in-depth conversations with everyone. This may be done in some congregations, but there are other ways to make general assumptions about interests. One way is to look at a person in terms of the life cycle.

A person in the mid-thirties has vocation and career in

mind. He or she may also be concerned with small children, a marriage, or establishing a residence. Any of these areas may have interests. A person in the fifties will have some clear-cut hobbies or interests that should be evident in conversation. Life cycles are important determiners of interests.

Personal crises promote interests and may lead people into volunteer work. Giving birth to a child with a congenital problem may lead some persons to devote considerable energy to organizations or interpretation of research on this problem. Such an individual would be an invaluable program and personal counseling resource in the church.

Dealing with an elderly parent or becoming a senior citizen may provoke volunteerism among some. Aging is not an easy process. A person willing to learn and help others can be a major asset in a church.

Concern by a parent about teen-age pregnancies may involve such a person in working with unwed mothers or developing programs for youth around the issue of human sexuality.

Any number of life experiences spark interests that can involve persons in volunteer activity. Keeping in touch with people is the major requirement in interest recruitment. Knowledge about life-cycle needs will be a help in knowing general interest areas.

Interests and concerns change according to life changes and vocational changes. The recruiter is aware of this. It is safe for a recruiter of volunteers to work on the principle that people are always changing. This principle means that two or three options for volunteer activity are given to all those contacted. These options ought to cover a spectrum of activities. The door should be open for the individual's suggestion. If a program is not available that can use the interest at present, say so and do not promise a new program.

Clues about interests and personal needs are picked up in conversations not only with the potential volunteer but with his or her friends. A recruiter of volunteers will arrange opportunites for meeting and talking informally with a wide range of church members regularly. These conversations are the place for clues to be picked up and stored for use later.

Rest Periods

"I just want to rest this year. I have been involved in the church now for three years. It is time someone else took over." This woman is one of the stalwarts of the mission program in the church. Her comments stunned the pastor. She had worked well. She did not seem displeased. Perhaps he had done something wrong.

No need for the pastor to feel badly. This is not an uncommon comment. It is well known to persons who recruit volunteers. The reason for the statement is the practice of churches focusing on a few people. These persons, because they are responsible and faithful, are given job after job. They, in fact, are the faithful few in any church. The church feels it cannot exist, or at least would be seriously hampered, without such people. The fact is that in time the church must do without any particular individual.

Returning to the faithful few, they get tired too. It may be a clue when they begin to miss meetings and become less regular in church than before they took all the jobs. An inquiry about their change of habits may result in the individual's denial that anything is wrong. During the conversation, however, they let it drop that they are giving too much time to the church. They need a rest.

It is best to respond immediately. A person must be

growing in a volunteer capacity. If the load is so heavy that growth cannot occur, the person's interest will die.

Many churches use a tenure system for leaders. This is designed to limit an individual's service on a particular committee or board to two, three, or five years. A few churches have gone the next step and provide an opportunity for a person to be inactive for a period of time. A period of six to twelve months is required before being asked to serve again. This guaranteed rest for volunteers is a welcome addition to a tenure program in the church.

What is a rest period? It is a time when a person does not have or is not asked to do any job in the church. There are no special jobs or short-term assignments made. This period allows the volunteer to get some perspective on his or her own activity, on the effects of volunteering on family or personal life-style, and the effect of their absence on the church. It also requires the church to find new persons. In a sense, it is a forced recruitment plan. The benefits to the church are fresh leadership, no entrenched group that controls programs or finances, and new program thrusts. Stability is assured by a staggered system of tenure. That is, only a certain number of volunteers are on "rest" at a time.

It is quite likely that after a rest of three to six or twelve months, a volunteer may be willing to reenter church activity. It is just as likely that such a person will choose a competely new area for use of time and talents.

Refusals

My wife recently informed me that she had agreed to become children's coordinator in the church. She had refused the position for each of three previous years. It was not that she had no interest; she had no time. Her work and having two preschool children took all her energy. Now, her schedule was a bit less hectic. In addition, the agreement provided that she could do much of the work over the phone. She had not refused out of unconcern but of personal need. When her situation had improved, she agreed so she could do a better job.

A refusal does not mean the world has come to an end. Neither is it a personal reflection on the recruiter. A no means that the *individual is not ready* at this time to take on the responsibility or responsibilities that have been suggested. This should not be viewed as a rejection of the church. People have needs and obligations they must honor. Not getting involved in activities at the church is one way of reserving time to meet their own needs.

It is common sense to keep in contact with the persons who refuse. Later conversation with such persons may reveal other areas of interest. Or it may be that a date for future involvement can be tentatively established.

Refusing to be involved should be viewed as conditional. Few persons write a decision in stone. People change and their needs change. Time is on the side of the recruiter. That is a prime reason for going back to those who refuse.

An example of what not to do is the minister who hates to recruit volunteers because he does not like to be refused. He almost never returns to those who refused, to ask again for them to serve. When return visits are made, the assignment is given to another staff member or to a volunteer. These persons are appraised of the original refusal. Sounds shortsighted? It is. People have good reasons for not volunteering at particular times. It is not the slight the minister feels it is, but rather a protection of things important to this member that interferes with a yes to the request.

A return visit to those who have been asked and refused is helpful to them. They continue to feel wanted and needed, two important feelings for potential volunteers. To be asked and to say no is helpful to the ego. "At least they thought of me." Not to be asked when one can do a job and is interested, even though other circumstances may prompt a refusal, is quite a different thing. It deflates the ego. "I guess they don't want me anymore." It is better to err on the side of showing interest and asking again than not asking and running the risk of injuring a person's ego. The church will need that person in the future.

Shy People

The world is made up of people who are shy. "I can't do that." "I could never be in charge of a meeting." "I don't know enough to teach." Every person who recruits volunteers can write a volume on "I can't . . ."

Experience shows that for most every "I can't" there can be an "I did it." Few people are truly incapable of being helpful. The difficulty is encouraging those who are afraid to take that first step. Such persons are afraid they cannot measure up to an imagined standard. They would rather be left alone than try. One purpose of the church is to help them become capable. That is reason enough not to let them alone.

There are stories of persons who changed from being very shy to becoming outstanding leaders. Those can be told by others. Yet one shy man stands out in my personal experience. He was a great hulking man who was certain that everyone could do anything better than he, especially if it related to the church. He did not really feel that way, but it was what he said. Consequently, he kept to himself and was very quiet.

As with other churches, we needed as many persons as we could get to serve on committees and help in the church. I approached this man and asked him to be a committee member. His interest and help were great. Within a few months, he was able to make his place as an important part of the committee and to assist in other jobs in the church. He did not become a public speaker. He did not stand before

43

crowds or even small groups. His contribution was as a committee member, and he gave considerable amounts of time to the church. Although shy, he increased in stature and value in his own eyes.

The key to this man was discovering his area of interest. It was then possible to put him with a group who were as low-key as he. He was able to fit in rather easily. He worked hard because the committee was responsible for major renovations in the building. He was a knowledgeable member as they examined bids from companies. It was not a glamorous activity for others, but it was a crucial service at the time. While his shyness prevented the church from having a new lay speaker, it did not prove to be a handicap in his work in the committee.

Every shy person will not assume responsibility like this man. The point is that most can become involved. Matching them with others who will not overpower them is important. Also important is not to attempt to make them over. The church is to provide them with an opportunity. It must be willing to support them as they struggle with themselves. Providing the opportunity is a ministry of the church.

Options

Every volunteer ought to be given options for involvement. This is especially necessary when recruiting the shy person. A request to become involved may be a shock to them. The result may be an immediate negative response. Yet, people relish the attention of being asked. It helps their image of themselves. They can respond positively more often if they have a range of possibilities. The first involvements generally need to be out of the spotlight. Later, many persons may be more visible in their leadership.

There are volunteers who appear to be shy until they are asked to do something. They change immediately and seek to take over almost everything in sight. Their worth can be diminished by their attempts to run the whole show. While they seem to change suddenly, these individuals usually give indications of their probable work-style during the conversation requesting them to do a job.

An example of this is the man who had worked hard for the church as a trustee for years. It did not demand a great deal of him. Consequently, there was no way to ascertain his abilities. He did much physical labor around the church and was cordial with the pastor. He was viewed as a man with limited leadership capacities. In time, this man was elected to chair the pastor-parish relations committee. In this church the committee was more a name than an acting group. When this man was chosen to lead the committee, he became a very strong-willed individual. He had gotten to a place of importance in his eyes and was ready to exercise significant leadership capabilites.

Persons like this may create surprises and even ruffle some accepted ways of functioning. So much the better. A person who is willing to assume leadership is to be commended. In this case, the man knew enough about the workings of the church to make positive and creative suggestions for change. He had served as an apprentice long enough to secure experience that would be useful in larger tasks.

A part of the reaction to the leadership of such an individual is the tone set by the pastor. A positive, supportive manner provides assurance. This tends to help the individual through those first weeks of "changing the world." In time, the person will be able to act more cautiously and responsibly.

Members Help Recruit
One of the hardest lessons clergy or staff of churches have to learn is to entrust others with responsibility. This seems

to be especially true when they deal with volunteers. Most laity are in situations demanding skills and use of judgment every day. Most are skilled in dealing with people. Nearly all of them must make assessments of others daily. Why not encourage church members to help find and recruit volunteers? They can be an asset in recruiting persons for the church.

One of the reasons for a consistent lack of systematic use of members recruiting members is a feeling that recruitment is the pastor's job. This signifies to members that they lack authority to ask people to serve. They do not see it as their task and do not want to encroach on the minister's job. In addition, most of them do not know all the jobs that are necessary for the church to do. Perhaps this is their greatest impediment.

Church members may be aware of the more obvious service opportunites like ushering, committee work, or teaching. Most members are less aware of other types of opportunities such as working with the elderly through home and hospital visitation, working in a mission enterprise in a nearby community, working with a family in crisis, giving time to answer phones in the church office, or other jobs that every church has available.

Yet another difficulty in members recruiting others is a lack of detailed information about each job. For example, if a person wants to be a teacher, what are the additional requirements besides preparing a lesson and showing up on Sunday morning? If a person wants to be a visitor in hospitals or homes, is there information about persons to be visited so that the caller may choose the kind of individuals he or she feels most comfortable with? In typing, is it done on a stencil or paper, and who provides the materials, and where must the work be done? Each job has details. Lack of information about them inhibits members from recruiting others.

One way to overcome the knowledge gap and to enlist members in recruitment is to develop and maintain a list of opportunities available to church members. Such a list contains a brief description of the task, the time requirement, and a contact person. An example follows:

Typist . . . Monday mornings . . . 2 hours . . . weekly . . . Contact Mrs. John Jones

C.S. teacher . . . 7th grade class . . . Sunday mornings . . . 3 months . . . Contact Bob Ward

Visitor . . . Pine Valley Nursing Home . . . Wed. afternoons . . . 2 hours . . . See Pastor Gill

Youth retreat leader . . . January weekend . . . Friday noon through Sunday noon . . . Contact Wilma Avary

Committee members . . . 1 meeting per month . . . 1 year . . . Contact Betty Key
    Stewardship . . . Education . . . Evangelism . . . Worship . . . Music . . . Ecumenical relations

Youth counselor . . . 4 hours weekly . . . Sept. thru May . . . Contact Pastor Gill

Choir . . . 1½ hours Thurs. evening and Sunday morning . . . Sept. thru May . . . Contact Mrs. Janes

Scout leader . . . 3 hrs. weekly during school year . . . See Bill Ward

Driver . . . for transporting choir members to St. Paul's Church . . . 3 hours . . . November 14 . . . Contact Mrs. Janes

Babysitter . . . Sunday morning . . . 1½ hours . . . 4 weeks at a time . . . See Bill Ward

The list would continue through the various opportunities for service in the church. It must reflect the total program of the church. Jobs are identified, contact persons are listed, and the time commitment is made known prior to any volunteer's acceptance of a position. The list must provide enough information for church members who want to volunteer, and also make it possible for them to begin suggesting persons for some of the positions.

The use of a contact person at the church relieves

members from approaching others directly. It gives them the chance to suggest with no obligation or need for further information. Since friends are aware of one another's interests, this form of recommendation assists churches in keeping abreast of possible ways to encourage members to volunteer. The advantage, however, is that the recommendation to a contact person at the church is regarded as a confidence. The recommender is not usually named or is asked if he or she cares if his or her name is used in contacting the suggested individual. This rule helps maintain friendships and frees the lines of communication with the recruiters of volunteers.

When recommendations are received, it helps to thank the one making the suggestion. It is useful to keep that person's name on file as a potential volunteer. A friendly phone call of thanks may provide an opportunity to raise the question of service.

Newcomer

A new face in some congregations is like the excitement of sighting land by the crew of Columbus. This is usually the case when a person or family comes three or four weeks in a row. The problem of finding a new church school teacher has a potential solution. The trustees, who need a new treasurer, begin to look anxiously at this person. The women's group, looking for several months for a program chairperson, thinks it may have found the individual.

Of course, the persons or families who happen to be the newcomers do not know about these designs on them. They came to worship. It seemed like a good church and so the newcomers have come back several times. They are sorting out their impressions at the same time the church leaders are analyzing potential involvements.

The newcomer syndrome, "get this person to take all open positions," strikes churches that have a relatively

48

small leadership group. This might be due to a limited membership base, or it may be a consequence of the recruiting-style in the church. Large congregations may rely on a small group to do all the work.

The syndrome hits churches with a small core of leaders in charge of the church. These leaders are rotated continually through the gamut of responsibilities. A few new persons are brought in now and then, but the small leadership does not vary greatly over the years.

When this happens, workers become stale and tired. Whatever fun and excitement they get from being a volunteer at the church begins to wane when there is no relief in sight. Their feeling of obligation is so strong that they cannot leave until someone else is found to take their position or job. The volunteer position begins to assume the demands of a regular occupation. At this point, relief is essential, and a newcomer who has not been approached about a position in the church seems the best alternative.

The program suffers in such churches because the easiest planning is to do it the same way as last year. Attempts at innovation are met with, "We tried that already." The membership may want something more but may not have the energy or willingness to break the cycle of rotating leaders.

The assumption that a newcomer is interested in getting involved immediately in a new congregation must be tested. If the person has just moved into the area, chances are that the person will need time to become acquainted with the various opportunities, including those through the church, in the new neighborhood. It will take time also to get settled. Usually during the first few weeks or months after a move, free time is at a premium. In other words, a newcomer needs an acquaintance time before he or she wants, or probably ought, to be too involved in the church.

On the other hand, some persons are so used to moving

that they seem ready to get started as soon as they step into the church. The church is their means of building a group of friends. These individuals may indicate readiness to volunteer for positions similar to those they held in their last church very soon after they move in. Even these newcomers, however, must have some time to consider whether or not the same jobs appeal to them in the new church. The church needs time also to size up the person and figure out where it needs those energies most.

Newcomers, as a group, are similar to members who have been in the church for some time. They come to the church for personal spiritual growth. They want to find a ministry they can perform. If a congregation tries to mold them into situations the church has need of, the personal ministry may be curtailed. On the other hand, the congregation has an obligation to encourage persons to volunteer for tasks of their choosing. It is for this reason that a plan of recruitment should be used.

Recruitment Plan

The plan of recruitment is a strategy for systematically enlisting volunteers for the church. It is used for all members as well as newcomers. It includes the listing of all tasks in the church for which volunteers are needed. This list is circulated to members of the church at least one time each year. It is updated and maintained outside the church office so that it is in clear sight any time people come to the church.

Announcements are inserted in the bulletin or newsletter regularly encouraging persons to sign up for a task. In a few situations such a list is a part of a regular visitation program. In this way, individuals are given an opportunity to express interest although they may not agree to a task at that time. This allows for follow-up contacts to determine continued interest and possible involvement.

An approach of some congregations is to use a talent survey card to collect information about potential volunteers. One of the difficulties in such a survey is absence of follow-through. People who complete the forms are not agreeing to do work; they are indicating what they can do if there is a task in the area of their competence. The expectation of those responsible for the talent bank is that people will sign-up for the kinds of jobs that the church needs done. The chuch leaders view the information not as a way to expand program options for the church by utilizing a variety of volunteer activities but as a way of identifying new persons to assume old resonsibilities. When the talents do not coincide with church needs, they are ignored.

A second problem is that the newcomer is a prime candidate for a talent survey. This is the easiest and quickest way to secure information about a new face. Unfortunately, the newcomer will have the same expectations after completing the card as do others in the congregation. That is, if I complete this card, am I expected to get involved?

The response may be, "No, not now. When you are ready, we are ready." By the time the newcomer is willing to become involved, several months later, the information on the talent card is not necessary. The area in which that person wants to be involved has been chosen.

In general, the talent survey is not a useful aid when persons want to become volunteers. It is helpful only when church leaders are interested in filling certain types of jobs. It is useful only when it is regularly updated, which takes a great deal of time and effort.

Identifying and recruiting volunteers is a two-way process. Church leaders know the needs for volunteers in the program of the congregation. They know also that members in the congregation are potentially able to fill all of those positions. As one person told his pastor, "Let us

51

know what needs to be done. We will do the job. Our problem is in not knowing what is needed."

One difficulty in operating a recruitment plan may be the organizational requirements the denomination imposes on a church. Programs are defined in ways that are clear to church professionals but often are not understood by members who want to become volunteers. How does one know if he or she has the ability to work in the area of evangelism? A recruiter or recruitment plan asks in a way that is simple to understand. It asks for persons interested in contacting new persons about the church, in trying to activate the inactive, and in helping think through and carry out projects for spiritual growth within the congregation. These are essentials of evangelism without the tag. People can volunteer for specific aspects of the total job.

The recruitment plan works because people want to help. Such a plan carefully used by church leaders gives members the chance to be involved. This is done by letting people know regularly the kinds of opportunities that exist within the congregation. The opportunities are clearly defined in terms of time commitments and obligations of the volunteer. Personal contact with the minister helps clarify the details of the task. This allows a person to determine whether or not he or she can fulfill a task on the basis of clearly defined parameters.

A caution to those congregations who contemplate using a recruitment plan. A congregation that asks for volunteers to fill positions needs to have all those positions available. In some churches, individuals are carefully selected to be members of the most prestigious and influential committees. While this may be justified on the concept of selection based on experience or expertise, after a while members of the congregation have the feeling that they are merely cogs in a machine rather than parts of an organism.

Church leaders are not all-wise. They do not select always

the "best" persons to assume leadership positions. Given the factor of human fallibility, it is important to include all opportunities for involvement, including those that are prestigious and demand expertise, in the recruitment listing. This may mean making a choice among volunteers, but this can be done rather objectively. When a recruitment plan is used, a new and exciting program is often the result. If change is not desirable and a large volunteer force is burdensome to a congregation, the recruitment plan ought not to be tried.

Chapter Three
Giving Assignments

A woman has agreed to duplicate the church's weekly newsletter. She hesitated for several months after her first indication of interest. Finally, she feels ready and a day is set. She shows up on time. The church secretary is busy with correspondence but nods and says she will be with the woman in a minute. The pastor comes in to greet and thank her for coming. He says, "I don't know how to operate the mimeo machine. The secretary will be right with you."

In a few minutes, the secretary completes her typing. She comes to the volunteer and asks her to follow. They go to a small room in a corridor down from the office. The volunteer sees, after the secretary unlocks and opens the door, a mimeograph machine and some shelves on which are inks and paper. The secretary asks if the woman has done mimeo work before. "Are you familiar with this machine?" The volunteer nods with some hesitation and adds, "It has been awhile ago."

"It will all come back as soon as you start. Here are the stencils. The ink is on that shelf, and the paper for the newsletter is right there. We need 350 copies. O.K.?" The secretary smiles and leaves.

If the volunteer were to follow her feelings, she would ask questions. She doesn't because the secretary is in a hurry, and the volunteer does not want to seem like an idiot. She looks at the machine and the room. Her misgivings about the job mount as she tries to figure out the working of the machine and how it is to be inked. She looks for the automatic counter so she will not have to count each page and discovers that it is an electric machine. She assumes, from reading the newsletter, that it is to be duplicated on both sides of a page. Where are the interleaves? She is lucky she has had experience. Even so, this is a bad start.

Contrast this with the experience of another woman who agreed to type, duplicate, and mail a newsletter each week. It is a new service in the church and can be a meaningful addition to the congregation's ministry.

The woman comes in at 10:30 on Monday morning to start the assignment. The minister is there to greet her. After she has gotten her coat off and is ready to begin, the pastor takes time to familiarize her with the office.

"The paper, carbon paper, ribbon for the typewriter, and correction fluid are on this shelf. On the shelf below are the stencil supplies. Two quires are on hand. By the way, if you need more, let me know. It will save time if you tell me when we have only one box left. If I am not here, make a note and put it in the middle of my desk top."

The woman nods. The pastor continues. "The correction fluid is here. The same process when we run low. The interleaves for use when we print on both sides of the paper are right here. There are enough for five hundred copies, which is more than we will run of most anything. For the newsletter, we plan 250 copies.

He leaves the doors to the cabinet open and moves over to the desk. "This is the typewriter you will be using. It is a standard electric model. This is the margin set, we usually use fifteen and eighty-five, but you can experiment. This is the tab. The ribbon position is this button. It must be on the white dot for stencil work. You will not need to worry about ribbon changes. Let's see. Oh yes, This is the on switch, and this controls the force of the keys."

Then he carefully laid out a stencil, took the time to help the woman put it in the machine and actually begin typing. Only then did he go into his office with the invitation to call if she ran into trouble.

Giving assignments to volunteers is an art of consideration. It requires a minister to think carefully about each step of a job. Most of these details have become second nature, so it is a conscious effort to think about them. It is easier to assume the volunteer knows something. While this assumption is easier, a more profitable approach is the exact opposite such as was practiced by the minister in the second illustration.

The assumption of a person who gives assignments to volunteers should be that they are not acquainted with the task for which they have been assigned. It is better to err on the side of too much rather than not enough orientation and instruction.

Giving assignments and providing instructions is like balancing on a tight rope between treating a person as a peer with sufficient experience and assuming that the individual knows little or nothing about a task. Even though a volunteer says that he or she is experienced in doing a job, it is safe to assume that their last experience was different than the current task.

The style of work in each office and church is different. Until the individual learns the style of this church or office, including where materials are kept, to whom to turn for assistance, and the most opportune time to come, the minister needs to be patient. Volunteering is putting oneself on the line and building an image of expectation with words that must be backed up by deeds. It is so much easier to be a volunteer when the minister and church staff are gracious and understanding.

In addition to patience and grace, there is a manner of giving assignments that create confidence. It is an art that can and needs to be learned. The following suggestions are essential elements.

Be Specific

A frequent objection of volunteers is that they are assigned to "Mickey Mouse" work that does not need to be done. They keep records that are useless or that are not used. Not only that, they must design their own method for keeping the records, or visiting, or tabulating attendance. There is often no rhyme or reason for their activity.

Such complaints are not found in churches where time and effort are devoted to identifying and describing tasks for volunteers. A few congregations use formal job descriptions which include a detailed outline for each activity as well as the reporting and responsibility procedures. This seems to work best for them.

This model is cumbersome for most churches. Many use a simple list of jobs. When someone expresses interest, the minister, or a staff member in a large church, has a conversation with that person. In this talk, the volunteer is told exactly what needs to be done, the amount of time it will take, and what support will be provided. It is informal and informative.

In both of these approaches to assignments, the minister's aim is to explain clearly and simply the nature and requirements of the job. The specifics are detailed and the reason for doing the task is clarified.

This is done at the beginning of the job so that the volunteer knows whether or not he or she wants to become involved with that particular job. Some will not want to do the job after this description. These persons may be given other options, or they may wish to wait a while longer before working in the church. In such a case they are thanked for their interest. When this type of withdrawal is made, the feelings of both the minister and the volunteer are protected. They have avoided an unpleasant experience by not continuing under unexamined assumptions.

In addition to knowing the specifics, it is important for volunteers to know the *why* of a job. It is usually clear to the minister why a task needs to be done. He or she should not hesitate to let the volunteer know the *why.* Volunteers want to see how their job fits into the overall program of the church.

This need is in keeping with the concept of volunteers expressing their ministry through work in the church. Ministry must not be wasted on jobs that have little impact on the life and witness of the congregation and provide little learning or witness for the volunteer.

Don't Lie About Time

A favorite tactic of a minister in a large congregation in the South is to say, "This job can be done in no time at all." Both the minister and the volunteer know this is a ploy to get people interested in specific jobs he would like them to do. It is an approach the minister has used for years. While the approach seems informal and cordial, the minister has considerable trouble in recruiting and keeping volunteers. The problem is that he lies to the volunteers about time.

People do not have unlimited amounts of time. They volunteer within constraints. That is the reason the approach used by another minister is more successful with volunteers. He tells each one how much time is expected, including the number of meetings for the particular job assignment.

Volunteering is serious business. It disrupts personal and family schedules. When it is clear how much that disruption will cost in terms of time, individuals and families can adjust in advance. They know what to expect. When there is no firm idea about time commitments, the disruption may become intolerable in a short period. Every volunteer must juggle church jobs into a time schedule with the other commitments.

A man was asked to help in the development of a dramatic production at the church. He was to work with the scenery designers and coach those who had difficulty with their lines. He was happy to do this since he taught English at the high school in town and regularly directed plays. The time requirement was identified as one night during the week and one evening on the weekend for a two-month period. As he looked at the schedule, he knew it would take at least ten weeks because he had had enough experience to see the unrealistic expectations of the church leaders.

He had not counted on the other, more frustrating problem he encountered. The people in charge of the production kept changing the rehearsal times. This meant that the young people who were to design the scenery and those who needed coaching were not available when he expected them. This resulted in several evenings of sitting and waiting while they were busy doing something else. As the event drew near, the frequency of the rehearsals increased and more direction was requested of him.

He had expected the increases in rehearsals but not the added burden of assuming more and more direction. He knew there had been no deliberate misrepresentation intended in the original request and time commitment. The leaders just were not aware of what was needed to get a group ready for such a production.

The man's commitment became a strain because at the same time he was involved in a production at the high school. When the church's demands were stepped up, he was caught in a time press. It was particularly annoying to have to wait for the youth. This was a result of the church leaders' inability to firm up their own schedules.

59

There are always times when plans for jobs are not farsighted enough. The result is a squeeze on the time of the volunteer. In the church, inadequacies in time-planning are harmful in the long run even though a particular event may succeed. It will be harder the next time, for instance, for this man and his family to agree to participate in another church-sponsored event. The feeling on their part may be that the price of such involvement may be greater than they wish to pay.

Such results are not inevitable. They can be avoided if the minister, and church staff members, and the volunteers go carefully through each phase of a job to determine the time costs. While they may not be able to estimate accurately the amount of time needed for each period, the minister can alert the volunteer to possible increases. The minister can be ready also to keep the commitment of the volunteer at the agreed level by assuming a greater role in the event or finding others to help. When both the minister and the volunteer are aware of the possibilities of time overrun at the outset, there is less chance of serious frustration and possible alienation.

A primary consideration in giving assignments is to adjust the demands of the job to the time availability of the volunteer. When this is not done, an individual may get into the job only to feel overloaded as time demands increase. Then that person stands a good chance of being unable to do an adequate job. This can result in a feeling of diminishing returns as he or she spends most of a week in a church task, especially if the original assumption was that only a few hours would be needed.

When jobs cannot be trimmed, it may be possible to find two or three volunteers to share the work. This allows the volunteers an opportunity to divide the various responsibilities between them. It also helps volunteers to schedule their own time while still meeting deadlines.

The aim of this tactic is to help the volunteers do a job in the amount of time they can give to the church. This, of course, assumes that the minister is aware, candid, and willing to adhere to the amount of time agreed upon to complete the task.

What Is the Minister's Role?

A closely guarded secret in one eastern congregation is the role of the minister when it comes to committee work. That is, is the minister going to see that minutes are completed following a meeting? Is this the responsibility of the chairperson or secretary of the committee? If the latter, is there someone who can do typing and duplicating? Such questions are not answered, or even raised, when a person becomes a committee member in this church. The information becomes available only when someone asks specifically about these things. In other words, offers of assistance are not a regular part of the recruitment and training of committee members. It is little wonder that volunteers are hard to recruit in this church.

For every job in the church, the minister or a staff member ought to be supporting the volunteers. That is, the minister is available, concerned, and helpful. Volunteers need to know that this is the case. They also need to be aware of the specific role of the minister in each job.

For example, if the volunteer is a treasurer, the minister needs to let that person know if it involves counting money after collections, if it includes all the funds in the church, or if it deals solely with the current expense check-writing and accounting. The minister needs to give the volunteer an exact description of the job and tell the treasurer that he or she can expect the minister to ask for a review of the books regularly, to want a written report every month for board meetings, and to call occasionally for information about certain items. This is the kind of information that is conveyed in personal conversation and in writing. In this instance, the minister's role is to assist the treasurer in keeping accurate and up-to-date records.

A volunteer who understands his or her job plus the role of the minister can decide quickly whether or not he or she wants to be involved. A volunteer will do a job best when he or she knows that the minister is behind that job and can and will assist at any hard spots. The volunteer will become disinterested in the job when a minister dictates the way a task ought to be done and then tries to take the job away by assuming more and more responsibility.

A certain minister in the Midwest cannot let go of responsibility. He wants to work with volunteers, but his manner is to treat them as small children who cannot follow through on a job. He is afraid of letting them be creative. He gives volunteers vague instructions about jobs and creates a feeling on the part of the volunteers that they will make important contributions. The illusion is dissipated quickly. The minister spends a volunteer's time telling him or her exactly what to do or taking over the job and reporting the results to the volunteer. Needless to say, it is very discouraging and frustrating to those volunteers who want to accomplish something in the name of the church. The minister aborts an opportunity for their ministry.

Most ministers will deny that their methods are in any way like this. Unfortunately, few ministers can be objective about how they deal with volunteers. It is reasonable to suspect that many ministers have a tendency to act like this one. After all, ministers are ultimately responsible for seeing that the church does have a program. It takes much trust and willingness for the clergy to allow volunteer workers to deal with the problems they encounter as they work through the church. The wise minister, however, has the grace to support but not take over from volunteers during difficult times. Such ministers build strong corps of competent and willing helpers.

A part of any success in maintaining a large group of volunteers comes because at the start of each task the volunteer and the minister are clear in their understanding of their respective roles in the job. Expectations are clear. When there is some difficulty, both can refer back to the original ground rules.

The best way to establish and maintain ground rules is to write them down. A listing will be helpful as a reminder of the agreements and responsibilities of each person throughout the task. The list will be helpful to the minster in keeping straight the kinds of supportive relationships that must be maintained with each volunteer.

Fences and Boundaries

In one part of southwestern Massachsetts, the fields are marked by stone fences. They are a beautiful sight as they run up and down hills and into forests. But this beauty is a by-product. It is not what they were built for. Those fences are there to separate properties. They mark the limits of individual ownership.

Jobs in the church are quite different than the pastoral scenes of Massachusetts hills. They are not different, however, in the need to have clearly developed boundaries. Indeed, each job has its own limits whether these are stated or not. Sometimes these must be discovered by a volunteer and may cause embarrassment, hostility, or lost time, or all of the above. It is for this reason that a minister ought to alert each volunteer to any limitations in a job before work is begun.

A young man volunteered to duplicate the Sunday bulletin in a church. The minister was near retirement and happened to be quite ill. As the year progressed, the young man took more and more responsibility not only for the bulletin but in developing the Sunday morning service. The congregation was not aware of his assumption of the minister's roles. It came to light only when another minister came into the church. The young man had become attached to his responsibilites and was quite reluctant to allow the new minister to assume any of the normal responsibilities related to selecting hymns, prayers, and the order of worship.

By stretching the boundares of the original job, the young man created, in the long run, a confrontation between him and the new minister. It was an unnecessary situation but one that is not unusual.

A church in a northeastern city had a young man as a custodian. He was partially crippled, but this did not keep him from doing any of the tasks at the church. He was a bit slow, but he kept the church maintained. As time went by, the young man developed a proprietary attitude toward the church. He began to determine who was going to use the building and when. The trustees were not a strong group, and they were often overruled by this man who controlled the builing with his key and by his personal authority.

The situation seems preposterous, but this young man had expanded the fences of the janitorial job so that he became the maker of building policy. The inevitable clash came when the trustees elected a new president. Not too many months passed before a confrontation, and it created nothing but ruffled feelings. It also resulted in a new janitor and even caused a split in the church.

These are situations that could have been prevented. The jobs assigned to each of the young men were given with very casual understandings about their responsibilities. There was nothing in writing, nor were any records kept of what these jobs entailed. Neither was there any follow through by the ministers or the committees to make certain that the jobs were being done within established guidelines.

In both instances, the jobs were given with no official limits. Consequently, each young man was allowed to do his own thing. They kept assuming more and more power. The ministers and the committees failed to act because they did not know the original limits of the agreements, and they "did not want to hurt anyone's feelings."

Robert Frost felt that the best way to keep a neighbor is to have a nice secure wall defining the common property line. The best way to maintain volunteers is to establish the limits of their responsibility both for their sakes and that of the church. People are not usually greedy for power when they volunteer. They want to get involved. They are concerned about the church. In time, some come to feel a responsibility to fill gaps they see in authority and policy, even when they have not been requested to take on additional tasks. It is essential to make certain at the outset of the limits of authority for each job. It is equally important to follow up regularly to see the fences have been maintained.

There are boundaries other than responsibility. These may be time limits. For example, a Sunday bulletin must be done in time for use at the service. When it is ready two or three days in advance, tempers can be kept cool. If a volunteer is to do the bulletin, the deadlines and contents must be clear.

Other kinds of limits have to do with spending money for supplies, determining group size, establishing age group-ings in church school and youth activities, and use of the church building. Each church has policies, or at least practices, which regulate each kind of task for which people volunteer. It is helpful to have the jobs listed along with their limits as established by a board in the church.

Developing such a list may seem unnecessary, but experience indicates that in working with people, it is a good thing. Volunteers come and go, but the limits to the tasks remain. If a list is made, it can be maintained easily.

This list in the long run will enhance working relations. It will provide volunteers with assurances of what they can and cannot do. Such limits provide a degree of security to persons, and especially to volunteers.

Work Plans

Much is made of planning in this book. Plans are an essential form of conserving time and energy, two commodities in scarce supply for both volunteers and ministers. Time spent carefully at the beginning of a job can save hours of wasted motion during the job itself.

The development of work plans is done cooperatively by the volunteer and the minister. Planning comes after the task has been set forth clearly, the limits have been agreed on, and the general deadline set. The next step is to schedule the work so that it can be done within the time limits.

The experience of the minister or a staff member can be very helpful to volunteers in planning. For example, a person has agreed to be in charge of a church dinner. The minister can help the volunteer plan for the recruitment of others to do the cooking, serve the meal, set up and decorate the hall, publicize the event, sell tickets, and take tickets. These plans will be made several months in advance of the dinner so that an optimum number of persons may be served. Even an individual who has been in charge of such dinners several times will be helped in planning by a minister or another individual who has experience.

The point of the minister being involved is twofold. In the first place, he or she brings expertise based on experience to most tasks in the church. Even if there is no experience in a particular task, the minister can recommend others who can assist at various stages of any job. The second reason is that the minister knows what else is happening in the church

66

and can suggest timing and availability of persons to help in various aspects of the job.

It is not necessary for the minister to be present in all planning sessions. Some volunteers require more than a single session. The important thing is that the minister have an opportunity to look through the plan carefully before the work is begun.

Some persons are experienced and can develop their own work plans. They require little assistance but still need the checkpoint with the minister prior to starting work. Others who volunteer are neophytes. They must be helped in the total planning process because they lack experience. These persons will take a considerable amount of time and attention from the minister not only at the beginning but during the job. Their confidence will not be great enough for them to do too much on their own without checking back several times with the minister.

Planning sessions are opportunities to train and counsel. These times ought not to be looked upon as interruptions to normal ministerial activities. They are periods of personal contact that can broaden understanding of individual needs and possibilities. Ministry is a keynote in such sessions.

Time Tables and Check Backs

Planning is identifying and defining the various steps needed to do a job. Included in the planning phase of a job is setting up a time table. In a manner of speaking, each job has a PERT chart (time and task schedule) that includes the calendar deadline for getting each phase done. This helps a volunteer know at the beginning of a job how missing a deadline will cause consequences on subsequent steps.

Human nature is predictable. It looks for the easy out in any situation. Only self-discipline can overcome the tendency people have to let things go until the last minute and then to make a hurried, superficial effort. Volunteers are no more nor less likely to be afflicted with a large dose of procrastination than ministers or church staff members. It is good, therefore, for both to have checkpoints in their schedules.

Checkpoints are not there so that the minister can see how well or how poorly a volunteer is doing. They are in the schedule so that both parties may be reminded of mutual obligations in finishing a job. Usually there are tasks that both need to do along the way that will result in a finished job for the volunteer and a planned use of the results by the minister or church leader.

A man was in charge of planning, organizing, and conducting an annual stewardship campaign in the church. The pastor decided to let the man do the job without interference. This meant that the minister did not help set up a schedule, did not establish checkpoints or assist the man in planning the total task. After all, the pastor reasoned, the denominational guides for the stewardship campaign contained detailed helps and a calendar.

The campaign director ran into one problem after another. Recruitment of assistants was nearly impossible since he did not know them well, and they were not approached by the pastor. Furthermore, it appeared that the director did not have the strong support of the pastor. Unfortunately, the minister did not understand his role as *legitimator* of the entire process. He thought he had done enough by getting the director.

The director also had difficulties with the calendar. The denominational outline called for a process of thirteen weeks. This man had only eleven weeks available because he had scheduled a vacation tour with his wife. In addition, the two or three weeks before the trip were especially trying at work. It was precisely at these points that the most time was demanded in the campaign. The director did not know how to cut the time down or how to adjust the schedule to relieve himself of much of the responsibility during these critical visitation and commitment stages of the campaign.

The campaign was a disaster. The training of visitors was poorly done. Commitments were down. Members in the church were unhappy because the church program was not presented clearly. The budget was only slightly changed from the year before.

Who was to blame? The pastor. He had recruited a person to do a job without clearly spelling out his own role as pastor. He had not helped the man plan or develop a time schedule. If he had done so, the pastor would have known months in advance the heavy time demands during the latter stages of the campaign. The pastor could have gotten someone to replace the director or at least to serve in a joint capacity with him.

There is no feeling of interference by a volunteer when a time schedule is established with checkpoints identified. Indeed, the checkpoints become the bulwarks against such disasters as this church experienced.

What was the long-term result of the pastor's desire not to interfere? The man who had done his best felt like a total failure. He lost prestige in his own eyes as well as those of the church members. He refused to accept any other leadership or volunteer position in the church. He had had it with the church. The situation could have been changed entirely if the pastor had been willing to plan and check back regularly with the man. The church lost a worker because of the minister's negligence.

The consequences of not setting realistic expectations are much greater than those of "interfering" through periodic checks on a person's progress with a task. Of course, a feeling of interference will be much less if the volunteer knows *why the minister is making the checks.* When the *why* is seen as mutual concern for the total program of the church, it is viewed as legitimate. If the minister insists on checking

69

back as a means of prodding the volunteer, chances are that the worker's reaction will not be very positive. Prodding begets resistance. Concern encourages a desire to do well. Establishing a schedule with regular checkpoints shows concern.

Providing Resources

The man in charge of the stewardship campaign was given resources that were called for by the manual. The manual itself was a major resource which outlined in a step-by-step way the procedures for setting up and carrying out a campaign. The one resource that was essential he could not get. That was the pastor. The person who could legitimate him and make his work in recruitment and training much more effective and efficient was not available. Without that resource the man was doomed to failure.

A church organization was contemplating revising its structure so that it could make better use of its staff. The restructure suggestion was that the organization use work groups rather than remain in the more rigid departmental pattern. This did not eliminate the need for either managers or technicians, but it did give them more freedom to work together. The suggestion was greeted with, "We do that now. That's not a change."

Further discussion revealed that indeed the organization did use work groups across departmental lines. What they had not done was to label their method. Every time they worked together it was informally as friends, without feeling they had the kind of authority within the group that they had in their separate departments.

Legitimation, the approval of a person or an activity by the person in charge, usually the pastor, is a necessary resource for volunteers. It is improtant not only for their own understanding of the job, but it is crucial when they are trying to accomplish something in the name of the church.

They need to be approved and supported publicly by the minister.

A phone call from a volunteer asking an individual to lead an adult class is important. A phone call from the pastor asking the same question is more important. While a minister may say this is untrue or the case only in specific situations, volunteers know by experience that the minister is a helpful resource in most every phase of a job. In this sense, the first, and perhaps most important, resource offered to a volunteer is the backing of the minister.

The minister will determine for each job and each volunteer what is needed to make their job easier. This is more obvious for some tasks than others. For example, teachers need materials, books for both themselves and the students, and training. Treasurers need record-keeping books, reporting blanks, and deposit slips.

It is less evident what resources a home visitor needs. Some training, perhaps; a few pamphlets. What are other things that may be needed? Confidence is essential. This may mean that the new visitor accompanies an experienced one a few times before going it alone. Knowledge about the person or persons to be visited is another need. This can be met by talking with the minster or sharing nonconfidential information. Another need may be transportation. The volunteer may need some help in getting to or from a visit.

Each job has its resource requirements. They are not always obvious or quantifiable. The sensitive minister will try to provide the essentials at the outset, and then provide support in other ways during a volunteer's time on the job.

Results

The jobs done by volunteers in the church will have a multiplicity of results. Their efforts will affect the number of persons coming to a dinner. They will help determine the number of pledges and the amount of money underwriting the budget. Their efforts will certainly be related to the number of new members in a congregation because of volunteer visitation. They share responsibility for the number of calls a member receives during an illness.

Immediate results are to be hoped for but should not be expected. For instance, one minister was astounded when a couple walked into the church one Sunday morning. He had had a disagreement with the couple three years before and in subsequent calls had found the reception frigid. In fact, he had not called upon them during the past year. He nodded and smiled as they returned his greeting.

As they were being seated, he went over to one of the ushers. "It is nice to see Mr. and Mrs. Drumond in church today." The usher nodded but did not say anything. The pastor was left to puzzle over the situation.

He made it a point to call on the couple the next week. He was amazed at the cordial welcome he received. During the visit, he tried several times to bring himself to ask what had led them back to the church. At last they brought up the subject. "I guess you are wondering why we came back to church?" Without looking too eager, he said, "I am a bit curious."

"One of the ladies in the church saw us the other day at the market. She went out of her way to be nice to us. Then she came by the house later in the week saying that she was visiting a shut-in in the area. Her concern and manner were great. It made us think that maybe we were to blame for the problem we had had with the church. We decided to give it another try."

This volunteer did not know she was a reason for the couple's return to the church. She was doing her visiting and had stopped by for only a few minutes. It was a spur of the moment stop to her. In this instance, the result was immediate, and it was unexpected.

These kinds of things happen occasionally. They occur

only when a volunteer feels an appreciation for the church and a willingness to speak out for it. These volunteers know that any results of their work will be appreciated. Thus, this woman was quite secure in her feeling that visiting this couple would not be frowned upon by the pastor or any other church leader. She knew they would accept her activities as legitimate.

This is a hard lesson for some ministers to learn. They have in mind the kinds of results they want from each job. When that result is not forthcoming they are disappointed and may not use or even acknowledge the efforts of the volunteer. A wise minister allows volunteers leeway in developing and doing a task. This minister knows that everyone approaches a task with somewhat different interests and goals, and that the results from most endeavors of volunteers are usable and can be quite helpful to the church. Even when conflict is aroused, this can be channeled constructively. Such a minister is a joy to work with and will be open to unexpected results.

Volunteers should not be countermanded or ignored when the results of their tasks are not to the immediate liking of a minister. Minsters should try their best to be open to change and not to be defensive about their own status and role. The use and appreciation of the results of a volunteer's efforts may call for ingenuity at times. Nevertheless, the volunteer has given time, and the results need to be taken seriously. A good minister never forgets that.

Chapter Four
Helping Volunteers Plan

"What this church needs is a plan. Something that will keep us on track; some goals so that we know when we have accomplished something." The speaker sat down amidst a burst of applause. The meetings of the board in this church would no longer be the same. The call had come for a plan and goals for program.

"Could you tell me when and how to get people trained? I know the *why* and the *where.*" The plea to the pastor was from a young woman recently appointed as children's department head. She wanted to do a good job but needed help in planning from the pastor.

Regardless of the task, a person must plan to get it done. Since pastors and other church staff or leaders are responsible for helping volunteers, it stands to reason that one of the most important contributions will be in helping volunteers plan. A purely selfish motive might be behind the help since planning is the best way pastors have to save time and energy when working with volunteers.

Planning is looking at a task and breaking it into smaller more manageable components. It assists people to think through the schedule needed to complete a task. Most important from the point of view of volunteers planning begins with goals toward which they are aiming. The goals relate each task to purposes critical to the existence of programs in the church.

A plan is built by volunteers and the pastor. It is not participative so much as it is cooperative. The difference between the two is that cooperative planning requires preplanning by the pastor who develops the basic plan including the schedule and checkpoints. Then, he or she and the volunteer cooperatively work out the details and come to an agreement on all phases and activities contained in the plan. Participative planning means that no preplan exists, and the pastor and the volunteer do the whole thing together. This type of planning is usually not necessary and is too time-consuming for most jobs in the church.

Regardless of the type of planning used, each job a volunteer undertakes requires joint planning with the pastor. It is not an optional activity. It is a necessity. It is a discipline. The dividends are significant, especially to pastors or church staff members who work regularly with volunteers.

A Planning Process

Everyone uses a planning process of sorts. The need lifted up here is to formalize a process but keep it simple. One such process consists of four steps.

1. Identify Purposes.

A planning process begins with the establishment of purposes. These may be quite limited, as in the typing of a newsletter. Or they may be extensive, as in the case of visiting to help renew a member's commitment to the church. Regardless of the scope of the tasks, each has a reason for being included in the total program of the church. Listing this purpose is the starting point for planning.

2. Establish Goals.

The next step is to establish goals that will meet the purpose. A goal, for example, might be that each

Wednesday by noon the newsletter will be typed, duplicated, and in the mail. This goal presupposes the attainment of other goals such as the deadline for receiving materials to be included in the letter; making certain that the persons responsible for typing, duplicating, and mailing do their jobs on the prearranged schedules; and having someone take the letters to the post office by noon on Wednesday. Each of these jobs has other tasks dependent upon it. The goals for each job must be specific, clear, and deadlines must be established so that the other goals may be met.

3. Identify Resources, Personnel, and Schedule.

The next step in the process includes: identifying needed and available resources, such as money for postage; persons and a few alternates to do each job; the training and orientation that is necessary; and an agreed-upon time schedule. These are all a part of the planning for a task. They are critical to getting on with the job, but up to this point the job has not been started.

Experience has shown that it is easier to work out these details during a planning session or two than to try scurrying around looking for resources as they are needed later. In addition, as in the case of the man who had trouble recruiting assistants for the stewardship campaign, planning relieves the need to stop halfway through a project to look for and train individuals to help.

4. Implement Plan.

The final phase of the planning process is implementation. Each aspect of the job has been carefully outlined, and work can begin on schedule. For example, a person has decided to visit on Tuesday and Friday afternoons at two different nursing homes. The planning phase included marking on a map the locations of the homes, listing the church members in each home along with their general condition, calling the homes to find out the best time to visit, and putting together a packet of things for the visitor to take. Included also is a discussion on transportation to and from the homes. Finally, a church contact person is noted in case the volunteer runs into any emergency. Tuesday afternoon at 1:30 the visitor is on her way to see three members in one home. She is implementing the plan.

These planning steps are essential to the successful completion of each job. Some persons need more help in planning than others, but each volunteer will be assisted by careful and detailed planning guidance from the pastor or church staff member. Such a session is no time for skipping over the details. Small things turn out to be the most troublesome. All the details must be dealt with through the planning process. It relieves frustration and prevents lost time later.

The role of the pastor in planning with volunteers is critical, and needs to be emphasized. Experience has shown that the following parts of a planning activity are essential to increasing the effectiveness of volunteers.

Start with a Plan

Two approaches to planning with volunteers are often encountered. One is to begin as though the person has had no experience in a specific job. This approach is supposed to encourage creative thought. It is frustrating and time-consuming.

The second approach is to have a plan already in mind that is based on past experience. So far so good, but implementation can be troublesome in this approach. The existing plan cannot be changed or adjusted. The volunteer must do the job exactly the way it has been done before. Almost no job in the church needs to be done exactly as it was done previously.

77

The identification of these two extremes should alert church leaders to nonproductive planning approaches. Neither of these can be useful to the volunteer or helpful to the church in most instances.

The reason is evident to those who have experience in working with volunteers. An individual comes to the church expecting the pastor or staff to have some ideas and experience with any of the jobs that may be available. This may or may not be the case. Inexperienced clergy do not have the background to provide detail for some jobs. For example, a minister just out of seminary has seldom been in charge of a local church finance campaign from its inception to its conclusion. This inexperience, however, can be offset and minimized by using resources that are available.

For example, the minister can take the time to go through the manuals provided by the denomination. In addition, he or she can talk in person or over the phone with denominational stewardship persons and in this way compensate for inexperience by tapping other resources. If this is too cumbersome, there are other ministers in the area who can provide counsel. The same is true for most other tasks in the church.

The volunteer comes looking to do something but expects some directions. It behooves the pastor to learn about the job before the volunteer makes an appearance. This will alleviate anxiety on the part of both persons, and it will give the volunteer a feeling of assurance that the pastor will be a reliable resource during the job.

In those few instances where the volunteer is quite experienced in the job, the pastor should make special efforts to learn as much as possible. It is helpful to the volunteer for the pastor to be able to suggest alternative ways of doing things. Ignorance and inexperience are no excuses for a pastor.

Knowledge about a job will assist the pastor in developing an approach to it prior to a volunteer's acceptance. Such plans are tentative, but they are important. A volunteer must be free to accept or reject them. This option causes some pangs of defensiveness on the part of some pastors, but it should not. The role of the pastor at this point is to be a stimulator and to assist in organizing the work. The volunteer will ultimately have to find a style that seems to be most suitable for this particular task.

Creativity for most people is not dreaming up new ideas or methods of doing jobs from out of the blue. Creativity is learning about a job and relating it to past experience of knowledge. This is the way a person can develop practical alternatives that produce usable results.

Creativity for most people comes as they react to specifics rather than initiating plans. This is the reason for the pastor to have plans ready for suggestions, review, and critique. Such preparation helps the volunteer be a creative participant in designing the approaches to a job that will be most helpful.

Proposing a plan and being open to working out a compromise is the best method for stimulating cooperative planning. The process begins with a firm concept of the purpose. The goals are identified and can be discussed and developed, and the job is broken into phases or segments. Such a process helps the volunteer and the pastor work out a plan in a relatively short time.

Interest Development

A basic limitation on the type and breadth of program in a church is the availability of resources. In recent years in some parts of the church this limitation has been a lack of money. Inflation has created shortages of cash and has threatened reserves. One reaction of churches has been to cut back on spending by reducing staff or dropping programs or both. Since it is difficult to know which church programs to curtail, a series of procedures have been created to help in the decision-making process. One of the most frequently utilized techniques is priority setting.

The procedure is rather simple. It is to list all current and proposed programs. An official group of the church then votes on each item in the list as being more or less important. Each member of this committee is given a chance to vote on a limited number of programs, perhaps six. They rate these in order of importance. The votes are tabulated, and the program with the largest number of votes for the top spot is considered to have the highest priority, and so on down the line. Since dollar figures are attached to each program, the list becomes a basic budget.

Establishing priorites is in some ways a negative exercise. The official body of the church sets priorities, and the remainder of the membership is told what they are. This imposes limits of opportunity on the church that may not be healthy. However, at present this appears to be a workable method for some churches faced with limited financial resources.

A few congregations add a positive step to the priority-setting task. The entire list of programs, current and projected, is presented to the congregation. After an official leader tells what the board has done priority-wise, the members are encouraged to volunteer to develop programs that cannot be funded through the church budget. Not all of the hoped for programs are picked up, but enough are picked up to add dimension to the church's life. These congregations are able to expand their programs even though the official body set a limited number of priorities. While the pastor is required to give first attention to the priority programs voted by the board, he or she also assists volunteers in developing additional program areas.

A church on the West Coast found that by encouraging volunteers to take on programs in which they were interested, but which could have very little financial assistance, the congregation broadened its outreach considerably. One group of volunteers began to visit regularly in several nursing homes and hospitals. These visits supplemented those done by the pastor and allowed him to reduce the time he had been spending. The minister was able to use the extra time in other aspects of the church's outreach.

Other volunteers organized and found the money to support a teen-age theater group. The young people meet two or three times each week at the church, and the group includes not only budding actors and actresses but support crews as well. Incidents of gang vandalism and rowdiness have declined in the neighborhood. This latter may or may not be a result of the church program, but the volunteers feel their counseling and time with the teen-agers have made a positive impact.

A significant happening in this and other congregations, which encourage volunteers to develop programs along interest lines, is that such persons enlist other volunteers. If need be, they find money.

There are problems in these kinds of ventures. People may feel slighted after their initial enthusiasm wears thin, and they receive little further encouragement from the pastor. They may develop a project that conflicts in space-usage or people-needs with priority programs. Such problems can be minimized if the minster plans as carefully with these volunteers as with the individuals working on priority areas. Interest programs require the same detailed help as do priority ones.

Priority-setting is important. It can be necessary when there is a scarcity of resources. The same process can be a stimulus for program development if it identifies areas of concern that need attention but for which resources are not available. Congregations that encourage volunteers to organize such programs will find that several of the nonpriority programs can be undertaken. One of the lessons for church leaders is that their most important asset is not money. The people in the church, especially those who work through it, are its greatest asset. When such persons are encouraged to experience ministry through their volunteer activity, the impossible can be done.

The Leader's Role

Current management mythology suggests that planning should be totally participative and should result in a consensus. This is a myth. Planning is a procedure that allows people to be heard and to be taken seriously in program development. Good planning does not require that groups come to a consensus, but rather that they decide rationally between alternatives.

Every organization has leaders and followers. The distinction is clear when the issue of ultimate responsibility for the organization's performance is assessed. Volunteers are not blamed for many of the failures of programs in the church. The pastor must bear the brunt for failure. This may mean that responsibility for the total program may be diffused from the pastor's point of view, but for the congregation, the responsibility is pinpointed.

A leader is a leader, and as such has responsibility for planning and doing and evaluating. Decisions are made and consequences faced. Involving many persons in program development and implementation does not eliminate the necessity for some one to decide and to lead. This usually means the pastor in a local church.

The leader's role, primarily that of the pastor, has been identified as recruiter, supporter, planner, monitor, stimulator, and decision-maker. It includes training and evaluating, both of which will be covered later. In short, a leader helps create a program for the church and then uses his or her talents to find individuals to make that program become a reality. The leader does not sit back and let volunteers do all the work. The leader participates with the volunteers. Underscoring three role expectations of a leader may be helpful.

1. A leader makes decisions. When a volunteer needs an answer, the leader either provides it then or within a short time. A person who is in a visiting situation and needs to know whether an individual should be called on does not have time to talk things over. That person needs a decision of whether or not to proceed. The leader makes that decision on the basis of knowledge. It is not usually a discussable item. The volunteer can provide an opinion; the leader must make and live with the decision.

This need for decision-making is most pressing when resources are involved. The leader is required to know enough about the state of the resources in the church to be able to decide when additional supplies are needed. This does not mean he or she carries around a balance sheet and an inventory. It means, however, that current information is kept about resources and can be consulted readily. This information is also organized to be helpful when a decision needs to be made with a minimum of delay.

2. A leader counsels. Counseling is a part of the planning, recruitment, assignment, and checkpoint processes. At each step of the task, the leader is looking to help the volunteer better meet responsibility, do a better job, or to assist with other types of problems that may be encountered. While this is a way of significantly increasing the pastor's ministry, the counseling and learning is never one-way. The pastor can learn and be taught by volunteers.

3. A leader legitimates. This is the role that is overlooked often by leaders. It is the public approval and support of a person doing a job. Pastors are the professionals in the church. They are looked to for all manner of leadership. When a volunteer assumes a job, it is the pastor who ought to let others know that this volunteer is capable and empowered to do a job. Saying this once, however, is not enough. Legitimation occurs and needs to be reaffirmed frequently.

These three roles are listed because they may be the most fundamental for any leader. They provide the stability necessary to develop and maintain a good program with volunteers. They give the human touch to working with volunteers that is essential. Emotion and feelings are important as motivating forces for volunteers. These three roles deal with emotion and feeling, and in this sense, they are essential for continued good relations with volunteers.

The "Big Picture"

A teen-ager agreed to help with the lighting in a production being staged by a youth group in the church. At first, he had to learn about the lights and the electricity and the positions he would need to take at various times during the production. He practiced with other members of the lighting crew. He found it interesting, but it was not fulfilling. Then came the first full stage rehearsal. It was then that he saw his role in its proper perspective. He became aware of his part in the "big picture."

Jobs in the church can seem insignificant, dull, and repetitive. They may be dull and repetitive, but they should never be insignificant. One of the reasons for frequent changes in volunteers in essential jobs is that they do not see them in terms of the total church program. Typing a sermon on Monday morning may not be an exciting task. If the typist knows that this message will be duplicated and taken to invalids and persons in the hospital and on regular visits during the week, the typing becomes more than just routine. The typist sees this task as an important part of the church's ministry.

Each volunteer wants to do something worthwhile with the time given. A feeling of accomplishment is possible when the job being done is seen as a part of the larger life of the congregation. It is therefore important for the pastor during recruitment, and certainly during planning, to show how all the jobs are a part of the big picture.

This does not mean that every person holds a critical task. It does suggest that unless a job contributes in some way to the meeting of the purpose of the church and its program, the job is suspect.

If a volunteer is asked to do jobs that are ultimately for the personal benefit of the pastor or a church staff member this becomes apparent when the questions about their consequences on the larger program is raised. This question should be raised to protect the integrity of the volunteer as well as the pastor. A volunteer works for the church, even when inspired and motivated to give time through the efforts of the pastor. It is essential that each person be told how this particular job fits into the church's program.

Feedback

Planning with a volunteer is one way to develop the trust and confidence necessary for a good feedback system. Feedback is letting a person know how others feel about the way he or she is doing a job. It is relaying information and opinion from participants in a program to the individual in charge of it or of all programs in the church. Effective feedback is a two-way process which involves the volunteer and the pastor.

Some pastors and staff feel that feedback is a nice name for criticism. Not so. For example, a church member needs pastoral assistance. A volunteer visitor discovers this during the time he or she spends with the individual and then relays the information to the pastor. Meanwhile, the volunteer has made every effort to prepare the way so that the pastor can have a productive time of counseling with the person in need. This is feedback.

At its best, feedback is mutuality in ministry. It is a free flow of information from and to volunteers who work in the church. Gossip and derogatory information are not considered feedback, although there are special occasions when even this intelligence can be important for the pastor or a volunteer to hear. In certain cases, gossip can alert the volunteer or the pastor to possible danger signals.

Feedback requires trust and mutual respect. An organist in a midwestern church has a technique barely adequate to play hymns and an anthem each Sunday morning. The newly arrived minister is disturbed by the mayhem she regularly inflicts on the music. It is truly terrible at times and is not conducive to meaningful worship from his perspective. He decides to try and encourage her to find another job in the church as a means of giving her time.

He speaks to some of the members, a couple of choir members, and finds, to his amazement, that none of them is disturbed by this woman's lack of finesse. At last, he has an informal conversation with her, and she brings the subject up with the comment that she knows she is dreadful as an organist. She explains that over the years, she has maintained ties with this church because the members have allowed her to work hard at her music and she has considered it a way in which she can minister not only to them but to herself as well.

This is not a satisfying conversation to the minister. He feels as though he is caught in a conspiracy. He decides to keep quiet and wait for an opportunity to suggest her move. After several months he discovers that she is a tremendous asset as a counselor and an example to the choir members and to other members of the congregation. It becomes clear that her lack of technique with the organ is a small price to pay for the kind of ministry she is performing. Only after this discovery on his part are these two persons able to have free and open feedback on issues and problems that concern them and the church.

Developing the trust and mutual respect needed for constructive feedback takes time. Trust and respect demand that preconceived notions of ministry and competency be tested and revised. Expertise is not necessarily the most important trait of a person engaged in a volunteer capacity at the church. It takes humility and grace from pastors and church staff to accept the various kinds of ministry performed by volunteers. When they develop this acceptance, the doors to communication can be opened and a much more meaningful ministry can occur.

Summary

Helping volunteers plan is a necessary task. It requires pastors and church staff to do considerable amounts of homework before a volunteer ever shows up at the church. It demands a method for planning that is simple and direct. It is based on the desire to use the time of each volunteer effectively and constructively.

The rewards for good planning will be not only a better job but positive feelings among the members. This atmosphere of trust is important over the long haul. Providing much assistance to a volunteer without experience in a new situation will enable that person to take a more creative approach to the task.

Encouraging persons to follow interests and develop programs that are not a part of the original program of the church will strengthen the volunteer part of the church as well as increase its outreach. The dangers inherent in such additions can be minimized by identifying boundaries and keeping in touch with each volunteer.

The key person in any church is the pastor. His or her role deals not only with the mechanics of working with volunteers, but includes dealing with them emotionally. These are crucial for long-term work with volunteers.

Knowing how each job is a piece of the church's total program helps volunteers understand their importance and contribution. This big picture, clearly presented at the outset of any task, can assure greater effort and cooperation.

Developing the respect and trust of volunteers takes time. It requires openness to change and willingness to admit error. None of these are traits easily acquired. They must be developed by pastors and church staff as well as by volunteers. They are essential if effective two-way communication is to be maintained. Without good feedback, the ministry of the church, of the pastor, and of the volunteer suffers. The results of poor feedback are a lack of knowledge about effects and feelings toward programs and inadequate counsel regarding persons.

Chapter Five
Running Meetings

A man arrives at the church at 7:45 for what he thinks is an 8:00 meeting. No lights are on in the building. He tries to open the door but it is locked. He looks at his watch to make certain of the time and looks around for anyone who might be sitting in a car waiting for the meeting to begin. He opens the packet he carries and shuffles through the papers. Finding a postcard, he carries it to the street lamp and holds it so the light shines on the card. He stares at it as though memorizing what it says. He puts the card back into the folder and looks at his watch again. He walks up and down in front of the darkened church for a few more minutes. Then he goes to his car and leaves. It is eight o'clock.

A short while after he has turned the corner, another car comes up to the church and parks. A person emerges, grabs something from the front seat and hurries to the door of the church. Juggling the files he carries, the man finds some keys, opens the door, and switches on a light. The man, now inside, looks at his watch. It is 8:10. He breathes a sigh of relief as he says to himself, "It looks like I am not too late."

In a few minutes, several other persons come into the church and find their way to the room where the man is sitting at a table. Each is greeted in a relaxed and friendly manner by the man who is seated, evidently the leader or pastor or church staff member. By 8:15 there are eleven persons in the room. The leader looks around and remarks, "We're all here but Harry. I don't know what is keeping him, but we had better begin. We have a full agenda and will need all the time we have to get through it. If you agree, we will fill him in on what has happened when he comes."

The leader is oblivious to the fact that Harry is not there because he had been the only one on time for the meeting. In fact, the leader was the cause of Harry's absence. The leader had failed in his responsibility by not being on time. In this sense, the leader was not prepared for the meeting. He had not been there before time, nor had he made arrangements for someone to have the church open for early arrivals.

A most wasteful use of a volunteer's time is often the hours spent in church meetings. Several reasons can be cited for this situation, but the real problem lies not so much with the volunteers as it is with the pastor and church leaders responsible for those meetings. A major culprit is inadequate preparation on their part. A second problem is that church leaders, pastors, and staff frequently lack training in how to run a meeting. Without training, a leader can *ruin* rather than *run* a meeting.

Meetings do not just happen. They are called because a group or a leader feels that something must be done. This might be to plan a program, work on a project, or whatever. A leader, feeling such a need, calls persons together for the express purpose of doing the task he or she feels is necessary. This means that most meetings are purposeful and decision-making events. While there are other kinds of meetings, the following discussion focuses on church meetings that are essential to program development and implementation.

Purpose

A meeting is called for a purpose. This purpose may be to plan, to review an activity, to negotiate agreements, to hire or to fire people, or to look at resources. There are all kinds of reasons for having meetings. Each program group in the church will have its own. To a volunteer, the call for attending a meeting means finding time. It usually costs an evening away from home, or it may mean losing an hour or two from a job. Either of these costs is important. Indeed, the choice of attending is a decision of import not only for the volunteer but for the group asking for that person's presence. It is for this reason that each member of the committee ought to be aware fully of why the meeting is called. The pastor or staff person who is working with a committee is responsible for assisting the committee chairperson to be certain that a firm purpose is in mind before asking people to attend. If it appears that a meeting can be avoided and that the proposed meeting does not meet a particular need, the leader ought to cancel it. Such a decision is difficult for church leaders to make, but the consequences are more detrimental. Nothing makes people stay away from volunteer work like attending meetings with little or no purpose.

One of the first steps in preparing for a meeting is to have the purpose written down. This allows the chairperson and the pastor to think about it carefully. The purpose may be in the minutes of the last meeting, or it may be communicated to members in the call to attend the meeting. No matter how it is recorded, members of the committee need to know the reason they are meeting when they are called or are reminded of its time and place. This helps them put the meeting in their personal perspective. It allows them to rate its priority among the other things that must be done on that particular day.

After all, a volunteer is trying to work for the church with a limited amount of time. Other things are important and may be more important than attending a church meeting. Volunteers go through a priority rating in order to attend a church meeting.

Call to Meeting

When a card or letter is sent to remind members of a committee meeting, the items to be considered ought to be included. This list is the basic outline of the agenda for the meeting. Enclosing the list with the notice does two things. First, it alerts each member to the issues that probably will be discussed. Second, it shows that the chairperson has firmly in mind at this time the items that will be before the committee for discussion. It gives him or her a sense of preparedness and indicates what must be done as final preparation for the meeting.

Including the probable agenda on the notice card does not mean that other items will not be considered. It means that among all the issues that may come before the committee or group, these are the most important from the point of view of the leader. They constitute the reason for the meeting call.

Listing the purpose and the agenda items helps the chairperson and pastor assess the need for the meeting. The call to meeting with the listing is the second step in preparing to run a meeting. Preparation is being stressed because a meeting goes only as well as its leader is prepared. A chairperson who knows what must be accomplished can be a leader. A chairperson who depends on the pastor or a staff member to set the agenda and does not confer with him or her prior to the meeting is not a leader. The pastor or staff person in such cases becomes the leader of the committee by default.

Since people do not become active volunteers without hoping to accomplish something, the meetings they attend must be useful to the church. Persons responsible for meetings can assure their usefulness by following the guidelines below. They should help achieve meetings that are better and more productive.

Set the Time and Place

This seems so elemental that it could be considered trite. Not so. For example, I remember two staff persons who spent nearly forty minutes in two separate locations because they had not set and agreed on a place for their meeting. In addition, each one thought the meeting had been scheduled at a different time. This sounds incredible, but it is a true experience. Needless to say, it caused some tension within the staff, not to mention the committee affected by their snafu.

Meetings are not just-happened-to-drop-by affairs for volunteers. Meetings are structured occasions in which some type of business is transacted for the church. As such, they require commitments of time and energy from volunteers. In consideration of the work that must be done and the time spent in doing this work, a clear statement of the time and the place for a meeting should be sent those who are to attend two to four weeks in advance. A few days before the meeting a reminder phone call is recommended for a very important meeting.

A gripe of many volunteers at least sometime during their careers is that they did not know when or where a meeting was to be held. For example, a woman who had been a stalwart in her church rushed up to the church one evening for a meeting and could not find it. Being dedicated, she waited for nearly half an hour before someone called the church office asking if by any chance she might be there. When she got to the phone, it was the committee chairperson who apologized for not calling to tell her that the meeting was being held in a home. Could she still come?

This is no way to maintain cordial relations within a committee, even when the volunteers are experienced and dedicated. Whenever there is a change in a meeting time or site, the chairperson needs to make certain that all members are apprised of that change. It makes a difference between a volunteer's coming or not coming. It may make a difference in the long-term workings of the committee.

Changes in meeting times and places should not be made except in the most pressing of circumstance. People seem to have a penchant for getting a date and a time stuck in their minds. When there is a change, they do not remember as well and some may even become confused. Many people look at a reminder and commit it to memory. Some use a calendar. Whatever the manner, the first notice is best remembered. If changes occur often enough, that will tell the volunteer that the leader cannot really plan for a meeting.

Meeting Time Plan

A friend, several years ago, confided that he developed a detailed time-use plan for every meeting for which he was responsible. He gave each item on the agenda a specific amount of time. It seemed strange then, but the technique has proven useful over time.

A time plan may seem rigid to some people. It ought not be considered in such a manner. A time plan is followed by most good chairpersons. It is the only way to have a meeting that moves well and provides each person an opportunity to contribute.

A time plan begins with the starting and ending times of the meeting. For example, the meeting begins at 7:30 P.M. and concludes at 9:00 P.M. This means that the committee will have one and a half hours for doing its work.

One and a half hours is sufficient for most church meetings. Two hours ought to be the maximum for regular meetings. The reason for such limits is simple. Many of the volunteers who attend a meeting have been working all day. They are tired. A meeting of less than two hours, if run well, is adequate. One that is two hours or longer usually suffers from a lack of planning and/or a lack of leadership during the meeting.

A time plan should be arranged so that the most important items are neither first nor last. Items that will take only a little time ought to be scheduled at the beginning and at the conclusion of a meeting. This will permit the meeting to have a buildup of interest, some time at either end for latecomers and early leavers to slip in and out, and a period for some letdown from the meeting's highpoint. The plan is psychological as well as task-oriented. Thus, the main agenda items should begin fifteen or twenty minutes after the start of the meeting and conclude fifteen or twenty minutes before dismissal.

A meeting actually begins with a call to order by the chairperson. This is followed immediately by introduction of visitors or new members. Introductions ought to be brief, in good taste, and accurate.

The next agenda item is a review of the minutes of the previous meeting or a review of the purpose for the meeting if this is the group's first session. This can be done quickly if the minutes or purpose have been sent to committee members prior to the meeting.

The next two or three items can be factual reports that do not require discussion. These are followed by the major items of business. Each item preceding the main piece of business on the agenda ought to be allowed at least five minutes, but reports for information should be given a maximum of ten minutes. The major agenda topic may take upwards of an hour.

As the time plan is worked out, it is useful to list outcomes expected from each item on the agenda. This helps the chairperson make certain that the purposes of the meeting will be accomplished. It also gives him or her an opportunity to be aware of the time needs for each topic. In this way, it helps the chairperson think through each item in advance of the meeting.

A meeting time plan with expected outcomes may look like this:

8:00-8:05	Call to order; introductions.
8:05-8:10	Review minutes of last meeting; corrections and additions.
8:10-8:20	Two sub-committee reports; information, progress, plans.
8:20-9:15	Main business; discussion and final action.
9:20-9:30	Other items; announcements, items for future committee attention, next meeting date, time, place.
9:30	Adjournment.

With such a plan for the meeting, there is considerable pressure on the chairperson, subcommittees, and pastor to have themselves prepared. It also requires discipline within the committee during the meeting to keep to the topic under discussion and to reach whatever decision is appropriate within the allotted time.

During planned meetings, more can be accomplished in less time than people expect. Some will want to talk a lot since meetings are a form of fellowship. The chairperson will limit this form of domination while providing the offender with assurance that there will be an opportunity to visit following the meeting. He or she will also suggest that fellowship among committee members can be had ahead of meeting time for those who come early. A meeting is for making decisions, and it ought to be held to that task. When a chairperson fails to keep to the task, the whole committee is penalized.

A time plan does not mean that meetings are sterile or rigid. Every meeting creates its own personality as a result of the interaction of the members concentrating on the programs and issues that bring them together. The style of the chairperson is crucial to whether or not the meeting is enjoyable as well as productive.

Careful use of a time plan will convince leaders that most meetings can be run on time. There will be plenty of opportunity to consider carefully the contribution of each individual. A meeting can accomplish its goals and at the same time provide persons with a feeling of fellowship and comradeship.

A well-planned meeting enhances fellowship since it cuts down on extraneous activities and discussions. It also limits the monopoly of a meeting by one or two persons. These two benefits are a result of planning and will relieve the frustration volunteers feel when pastors or church staff ramble on and on or when a leader appears incapable of handling a meeting. The time plan is a way in which the entire committee can maintain its integrity of time and purpose.

Adhere to the Schedule

The motto of one church official I know is to "plan your work and work your plan." This is not original, but is the result of an important learning he had some years ago. In private conversation this man tells whomever will listen that it is a waste of time to plan if he or she is not willing to put that plan into effect.

It is relatively easy to plan. It takes time as well as some organizational ability, but making plans come alive is much more difficult. This requires discipline, a commodity that volunteers are often hesitant to exercise with fellow volunteers.

One of the problems faced by a volunteer leader is trying

97

to respect the right of all committee members to contribute to the discussion and decision and at the same time to maintain the committee on a time schedule. Experience has shown that most meetings involving committees are controlled by a few of its members. Seldom do all members make full contributions. Each has his or her reasons for remaining quiet, but there is no meeting in which each member of a committee is going to have an equal degree of participation.

The task of the leader, therefore, is to make it possible for all members to participate. This may mean asking some individuals to limit their contributions so that others can be heard. It also means that when decisions are needed, the leader will ask the committee to make those decisions without further delay.

One of the best committee meetings I ever attended was handled by a volunteer. He had organized the meeting in advance. He knew most of the people who were there, and he had had experience with some of the members in other committee settings.

He came to the meeting determined to be in control. He allowed discussion, thorough discussion. This man was not afraid to tell the pastor or a committee member that he or she was talking too much. He asked for feelings and opinions from those who were silent. He encouraged each person to express himself or herself. He stopped on time and suggested that the members spend some time visiting informally before leaving.

In closing, he invited anyone who wanted to, to contact him the next day if new information was forthcoming that could make a difference in the decision the committee took. He did not say that these data would change the decision or impede action. He indicated, instead, that if he considered the information quite important, members of the committee would be phoned, given the information, and polled without another meeting.

The meeting was also exceptional because the man adhered to his schedule. He had set the time of conclusion and was within three minutes of that time at closing. He covered each item on the agenda. He exercised discipline when necessary to limit certain persons in their talking. He made sure that each member was speaking to the issue that was before the group.

The contrast between that leader and the committee chairperson in another and very informal church is like night and day. In this other case, informal means that the chairperson allows conversation to move as the group sees fit. When it becomes evident that the time pressure is getting intense, he begins cajoling the committee with reminders that "it's getting late." When, or if, decisions are made, they are in spite of rather than because of the leadership.

This church has a problem securing and keeping volunteers. The pastor does not understand the difficulty. He feels that people "just aren't interested in the church anymore." He does not understand the multitude of time pressures on church members. He fails to see that people have more important things to do than sit at a church for three hours becoming frustrated because they are not getting anything done. Even when the pastor helps leaders plan, they approach the planning with the feeling that it is an exercise and not really something to be followed in a meeting.

People respect organization. They want to feel accomplishment. These two attributes go hand in hand with planning. They demand disciplined leadership during a meeting. It is up to the pastor to help each committee chairperson secure the training that will help him or her become a productive leader.

Work the Agenda

Every person who has been in charge of a meeting knows the pressures of time. That is the reason a chairperson, in the construction of the agenda, will note how flexible the schedule or agenda is *prior* to the meeting. Some decisions or reports can be put off to another meeting. These are checked on the agenda sheet with some sort of code. The items that the chairperson feels can be postponed are cleared with the pastor before the meeting. The aim is to schedule all program and administrative items so that ample time will be given for their full discussion before any final action is taken.

A technique used by a church leader in a southern church is to request that certain reports be printed for each meeting. During the meeting, when it becomes apparent that time will run out and careful consideration will not be possible at this meeting, all or some of the printed reports are distributed. The members are asked to study these reports and be prepared to take action at the next meeting. The reports are usually of an informational character but not always. Some are beginning ideas on projected programs, and others contain background data needed for discussion of major topics. Whatever they happen to be, and they are varied, each meeting concludes with the members taking a piece of paper home to study.

This illustration may seem to reveal a person who does not plan well or stick to a schedule. The opposite is the case. The intent of a meeting for him is to have more things to do than can be done. He has a time schedule that encompasses all items, but he has spotted those which may need more time than is allotted. He decides which of the topics are more important and which can wait. This is done well in advance of the meeting. He then requests written reports from certain people, papers or background items, to be available just in case.

This man works on the theory that people will work hard for a limited period of time. After that they need to have relief. He sets a meeting time of one and a half hours. He is willing to devote one hour of that time to a single topic. He is not willing to go more than ten minutes past the scheduled departure time. Therefore his technique of using written materials as homework gives him considerable freedom.

He can allow important items to be discussed carefully and fully. Conversely, he can get several things done quickly. He can keep the members involved even when they are not at a meeting. They have homework between meetings.

This technique will not work for everyone, but it works well in this church. Volunteers there feel needed and make it their business to do what is expected. The organization of meetings gives them an opportunity to be heard. They are responsive and responsible.

The illustration lifts up points for consideration. In the first place, the leader works out a flexible time plan. He knows which items need more consideration than others. He determines which items can be cut prior to the meeting and thus is not busily scanning the agenda during the last fifteen minutes of the meeting trying to decide which things to eliminate. He has contacted the persons who might be affected by these decisions in advance. They have available their reports or whatever, and he is able to preserve their integrity of work by distributing these as written items. It is not an ideal arrangement, but it has helped make this church very successful in terms of involving and attracting volunteers.

Close on Time

An education director in a western, urban congregation cannot get his meetings closed on time. The people who come to the meetings are vitally concerned about Christian education and are excited about the programs that their church sponsors. Unfortunately, they are not hesitant about being absent. They cannot afford the extra half hour or forty-five minutes he takes each meeting because he is not disciplined. He also has difficulty living with decisions that are not his own. His tendency is to try to talk the committee down when such a decision is made. This, of course, takes time with few benefits to the committee.

One of the cardinal rules of a good meeting is to close on time. People might resent a meeting when it starts on time, but very few will say much about its closing when it is supposed to. In fact, it happens so rarely in churches that when it does, it is noted as an achievement. This is because of an attitude on the part of church leaders that people will be or ought to be willing to spend a little extra time on church business.

What these leaders fail to comprehend is that volunteers have already spent the little extra time they may have for the entire week in that meeting. The church needs to respect the rights of its volunteers to relax.

A meeting time is a contract with the participants. Usually when a person breaks a contract there is a penalty. In the church, about the only thing that a volunteer committee member can do to penalize the leader for a long meeting is not to come to the next one. This defeats the purpose of volunteering, and yet not to protest is to cut corners in another part of life. It seems that the church ought not speak about disciplined living if the pastor and leaders cannot practice it with the time commitments of its workers.

Assignments

A minister in a certain medium-sized congregation is very good at delegating responsibilites. He knows every member well enough to be able to fit a church responsibility with the interest and capabilites of the individual. He prides himself on this trait in his ministry.

There is one little flaw in his system. He cannot allow the volunteers to complete their assignments once they are given. That is, if he asks a person to be responsible for visiting six members in a week, this minister visits those six families before the volunteer can get around to it. This means that the volunteer has nothing to report to the minister. Further, the members wonder why the volunteer is visiting at all.

If this type of thing happened once in a while, it would not be worth noting. Unfortunately, it is the minister's regular practice to do the jobs that he assigns to volunteers. Their capability and interest are negated by his actions.

What does this do to the volunteers? If they are persistent, after a while they learn to check with the minister before they begin to carry out their assignments. This, of course, is to his liking. They receive detailed instructions from him in how to get their job done. Rather than being a positive note in his practice, this preaction ritual is twisted to meet his needs.

The practice of checking allows him to direct the volunteer and to control all the work in the congregation. It gives him a feeling of being on top of the activities of every group associated with the church. The net result, in terms of program, is a very limited range of activites in a congregation that could support many more programs.

No one person can or ought to be in control of a multitude of activities. This is not ministry. It is insecurity. There is not enough time for a single person to control a church program. One cannot expend more energy than he or she has. The members of the above-noted congregation, faced with these restrictions, are frustrated. But they are willing to live with the minister because "he does preaching and visiting so well." They feel they can let their program bog down under his smothering influence since there are other virtues to his leadership.

Perhaps this minister and this congregation are well suited for each other. In the long run, however, the church will die because of a lack of training and initiative among volunteers. There is no ongoing excitement since this man demands no creativity or innovation among volunteers. In fact, he stifles creativity. He runs the whole show. The church cannot grow or be creative so long as he holds to his present attitude of not letting volunteers express their ministry through the church.

1. Assignments Are Opportunities. Assignments are opportunities for volunteers to do something purposeful for the church. It is what they want to do. That is the reason they volunteer. When they are deprived of doing church tasks that require their skill and time, they are denied the very thing that proves rewarding in their work in the church.

It is important for a chairperson to identify the various tasks that must be done if a committee is to achieve its goals. These tasks are varied and will use a wide range of skills. One task might be to contact the members for each meeting by phone. One person can take this assignment. Another job might be to make contacts with several persons in order to secure one or more speakers or resource persons for the next or a later meeting. This can be an assignment for one or more members. The list can be extended according to the purpose and needs of the committee.

The point of making assignments is to free the pastor and a few leaders from doing all the work of the church. It also increases the feeling among the members that they really count for something in the life of the church.

The time for making assignments is before or after a meeting. Even when a subcommittee is to be chosen, the chairperson would be wise to jot down some names, test these with the committee during the meeting, and then state that the final decision will be made at the conclusion of the meeting. This allows the chairperson to talk with the potential subcommittee members in a relatively private setting. They may feel more free to say yes or no without the potential of embarrassment in front of the entire group.

2. Assignments Must Be Clear. Job assignments must be given in clear and concise language. Usually this means that one person should give the instructions. The task needs to be defined and spelled out in detail so that the volunteer knows approximately how much time and energy will be required to complete it. It is essential in making the assignment to state when and where a report will be due for consideration and action.

A clear set of instruction is a must. "You know what I mean" does not do the trick. Only *you* know what you mean. It is time- and energy-saving to clarify the job before the person accepts or rejects the assignment. Again, the specifics will depend upon the job, but it is unfair to approach an individual with a task about which the recruiter is unclear. It is far better to hold back on assignments until they have been clarified than to get people involved in tasks that later prove to be unnecessary.

3. Assignments Need Monitoring. Monitoring of assignments is important. This is usually done privately, but it may be done by requiring reports at each meeting until the task is completed. When it becomes clear that an assignment has been botched, the chairperson and the volunteer need time together to straighten out the difficulty. If this is impossible, the volunteer must be relieved of the assignment.

A pastor or church staff member must take some responsibility for a poor job by a volunteer. It is the pastor

105

who gives the person a job, provides the instructions, makes certain the training is done, and receives the reports. When these responsibilites are not met, the volunteer can blame the pastor for a poor job. A volunteer expects help from the pastor. An assignment with no support is not helpful. It certainly is not a form of ministry. Monitoring must uncover these flaws in the pastor's approach before condemning a volunteer.

It is important to thank and recognize a volunteer for doing a good job. This is another part of the monitoring task. When this is not done, the volunteer does not really feel a reward or fully sense accomplishment. Again the pastor should pay attention to his or her responsibility in helping people feel they have fulfilled a ministry.

In preparing for a meeting, the chairperson ought to be aware of the possible tasks resulting from expected actions by the committee. This person will be prepared to suggest the kinds of jobs required and will solicit names of volunteers from the members. He or she will be responsible for making the assignments, giving the instructions, providing the training, monitoring the progress, and handling the results.

Minutes

The minutes of a meeting are a summary of the activity of the group. These should be sent to committee members within a week of the meeting so that the issues discussed and actions taken are fresh in the minds of the participants. When the minutes are sent three weeks later, the people who attended may have forgotten or may have become disinterested in the meeting activities. If the committee is to be lively and productive, the chairperson will see to it that the minutes are out soon after the meeting.

The minutes ought to highlight committee actions and underscore follow-up assignments. This puts on the record

106

what is expected to happen and by whom it will be done before the next meeting. In this sense, the minutes are a planning document looking toward future actions and activities. It is also a chronicle of past and a description of current activities. A good set of minutes will keep the volunteers involved in the ongoing life of the committee.

Minutes that are historical only need not be produced for a committee. A continuing committee or a committee with life will be dealing with events in the future a good bit of the time. The chairperson, in helping the committee look ahead, will insist on the kind of minutes that encourage expectations among its members.

Chapter Six
Training

The church's program exists because of volunteers. They express their witness to the gospel as they participate in various jobs in the name of the church. The pastor and staff of a congregation, by encouraging or limiting volunteers, determine the vitality and outreach of that church. When people are allowed to use their skills and talents creatively in the church, the congregation can become a witnessing community.

The major responsibility of a pastor in working with volunteers is to equip each one so that he or she can do an exceptional job at whatever task he or she accepts. Indeed, the church has this obligation: to provide the training essential for volunteers so that they may witness effectively. These persons must be able to do their task in the best possible manner. Their effectiveness and witness is a test of the training process for volunteers in that church.

The word "training" has several meanings. In the church, it has been associated with skills as well as with feelings and attitudes. The focus of the discussion in this chapter is discrete; it considers training to be the process a church uses to help volunteers acquire the skills and background necessary to perform each task in the church he or she chooses to do.

The process assumes that there is someone who can provide the training. Such an individual is a trainer, a person who instructs others or assists them in acquiring the desired skills. In local congregations the trainer may be the pastor or director of education or a member with background and training. When a congregation does not have such a person, a trainer may be secured from a conference, association, or national denominational board or agency. Most of these have staff members who can help in training volunteers, especially in education, steward-ship, and evangelism. It may be that a congregation decides that it will not use its own resources or those of the denomination but will choose to engage an outside consultant. Such a person must be familiar with the skills needed to function well through the church.

Regardless of who does the training, it is essential, and it must be based on certain fundamentals. A few of the more important ones are lifted up for consideration in this chapter, others have been dealt with in previous chapters.

Every Volunteer Needs Training

A dearly held assumption of some ministers is that once a person has worked in the church he or she knows enough without having to attend additional training or orientation sessions. These ministers look at training in a very narrow sense. They believe it is applying whatever experience a person has gained in other church jobs to the task he or she is about to undertake. While this transfer of experience is basic to training, there is more to being an effective volunteer. Training includes relating previous experience to current tasks, but it also involves understanding the nature and functioning of the church, its purposes and goals, the manner in which each job fits into the total program. For example, a person who has taught first-graders in the church school can transfer only a small part of that experience to a new job of serving on the worship committee. Training involves reorientation and commitment as well as skills.

A woman volunteered to be the treasurer of her Sunday school in a small, rural congregation in the Midwest. She had no experience whatever in keeping track of income or expenses for an organization. She had no idea how to keep records so that a report could be put together easily.

She told the pastor her problem when he made his monthly visit. They worked at it together. The training took a relatively short time. They devised a process she could follow to keep track of the income and the expenses so she could total the sums and report to the board at its regular meetings. These few minutes saved her hours over the year. Not only that, she felt competent and self-confident with her new-found skills. The pastor, by taking a few minutes to help with this problem, had helped her become more important in her own eyes as well as gain new respect within the church.

A faulty assumption of the people in her church was that anyone could count money and record how it was spent. The assumption was generally correct. The difficulty was that it takes time to maintain records suitable for reporting in a church. It is one thing to keep financial records for a family, but it is quite different to maintain accurate and up-to-date books for a church. Experience with the family budget may have been helpful to her, but it did not provide the training she needed.

This illustration should not lead one to believe that training applies only to those involved with finances or persons assuming their first job in the church. Not in the least. Training is needed by each chairperson of each committee, by persons serving as committee members, by those selected to be part of a planning group in the church, by an individual on a selection committee for a new pastor or other staff member, and by persons who serve in all other church jobs. The training should develop a state of mind as well as skills.

It is no secret to pastors that some volunteers who have had experience in the church need more training than do neophytes. The reason is obvious. These experienced persons have found ways to do their tasks with little regard to the consequences of the attitudes or performance on the total program of the church. In some instances, such persons are loyal and dedicated individuals who give great amounts of time. Yet their personal manner is not expressing a Christian witness so much as it mirrors self-imposed duty.

The church is a unique institution which has its own rules and procedures. It is a voluntary society. It is governed not by the professionals but by the laity. It does not operate to make a monetary profit. It is not an organization that remains silent and aloof on controversial issues. It is concerned with all age groups. It educates, socializes, and theologizes. It is unique.

When someone begins to become involved in the church, it is important that that person become acquainted with the way in which things are done. It is necessary to learn the operating style of the congregation and the pastor. It is critical to know the way in which voluntary organizations function under the law of the land as well as the law of the church. In short, the desire to do something worthwhile must be informed, channeled, and nurtured.

Orientation and review of the church and its purpose are parts of the training process. These need to be repeated no matter how long an individual has been a member of a congregation. In addition, the changing character of the church demands continuous updating for volunteers. Three pressures of change require attention.

1. Changes keep happening in the organization and in the

111

goals of a congregation. A church is not a static institution. It is alive, and all living organisms change. While some congregations may have the movement of a turtle, there is movement. Other congregations make changes quickly. No matter what the speed or scope of the changes, the point is that churches change. People who are working in changing institutions need continually to be aware of the implications of those changes for their particular tasks. Training is a means of doing this.

2. People change jobs in the church. Indeed, many churches insist on a limited tenure system that requires people to move out of jobs after a certain period. When people change from one committee or activity to another, they need to learn the new vocabulary, some different technique, and new procedures for reporting. This requires effort and time. That is why training helps.

3. Skills need to be upgraded. New techniques are being invented and tested continually. Many of these can make jobs easier or more rewarding. Some innovations have to do with communication or record-keeping. Others are advancements in the ways humans relate to each other. Regardless of the type of innovation, information about new ways of doing tasks ought to be explained, practiced, and incorporated into the volunteer's efforts in the church.

Customize the Training

Everyone may have been created equal, but each one is certainly different. There are differences between persons in rates of comprehension, in abilities to accomplish tasks, in the amounts of discipline they can exercise on themselves, and in the limits to their desire to continue to work in the church. These differences are evident in the rate at which trainees absorb whatever skills are being taught.

Public schoolteachers know that allowances must be made for individual differences in aptitude. For some reason, when teachers are charged with training volunteers in the church, they seem to overlook this fundamental. They feel that church people are either very dull or quite bright. Thus, they overinstruct or skip parts of the job that are critical to effective performance. Thus, the training and the work of the volunteer are both impaired.

It is impossible to take a large amount of time to train any single individual, or even a group. The pressures of time on both the trainer and the trainee make it difficult. On the other hand, to spend insufficient time at the start of a job will mean more time later to make corrections in the job. This makeup is much more time-consuming than providing prejob instruction.

1. Training as a Two-part Process

It is because of time and individual differences that training needs to be customized. While this is not completely possible, it can be done by breaking training into two distinct parts. The first consists of giving a group of trainees general instructions and information. The second is a period for more personalized attention. This latter part may include large doses of on-the-job experience for those who need much help and/or assurance.

The training program, including both parts, will take about one evening. It can be done for all volunteers on the same evening. The general orientation to the church and its programs will take the first hour. The second hour will be devoted to instructions for groups of persons doing the same jobs.

A two-part training event will require more than one leader. A trainer for each task will need to be available although the more personalized training can be staggered. That is, after the first hour, some groups may have refreshments and spend some time in conversation while other groups learn about their specific jobs. This process can

113

be repeated throughout the second hour. It provides ample opportunity for fellowship as well as for skill training.

When more than a single trainer is needed, the pastor or the person in charge of the training will meet with the leaders in advance. In this time together they will prepare in detail for the training session.

The first part of the training is designed so that every volunteer will receive a similar set of information. This includes a discussion of the place of the tasks or tasks in the life and work of the church, the quality expected from volunteers, reporting responsibilities, and time commitments. If there is a policy for reimbursing volunteers for out-of-pocket expenditures, this is included.

The second part of the training session will deal with the specific details of each particular job. Even so, it cannot provide all of the information each volunteer needs. The more detailed understanding of each task will take place when the volunteer actually begins the task.

In the instance of a woman who came to the church to assist with typing, the pastor took the time to instruct and show her what she needed at that moment to do her job. This will be done in the second part of the training session, but a review will be helpful when the volunteer comes that first day. Such a session will vary in length but usually will run about half an hour. It should not take an hour. Its focus is getting acquainted with the procedures in the church for this job, the location of supplies, the availability of resources or equipment, and those with whom one will work.

2. Interpersonal Relations

Training deals with more than skill instruction. It is a time to test interpersonal relations. The church depends upon its volunteers not only to do jobs but also to create images for the public and other members. During training sessions, a trainer can spot potential trouble in a person's manner that could make him or her less than effective in a particular job. The trainer can make suggestions about other tasks that might better suit the personality and style of that volunteer.

Any suggestions about changing assignments or holding off on an assignment must be done gently and in private. The volunteer ought not to lose prestige or personal worth during a training session or while engaged in a job. The integrity of the person is more important than a job. This integrity must be protected and nurtured even if it means privately encouraging someone not to volunteer.

3. Providing a Practicum

People ought to be able to practice their task before they are charged with full responsibility for it. This is the basis for the apprenticeship in crafts or the internship in medicine or the practice-teacher requirement in education. In each of these, the person works in the actual job situation, but does it alongside a more experienced individual for a time. It is a learning and a testing time.

When a pastor insists on this process, there will be some who become angry or will even leave. Do not be discouraged. If the task is important enough for people to give time to do, it is important enough to do well. It is the pastor's responsibility to help each volunteer learn the proper skills for his or her task. This is best done by being immersed in the job with the support and assistance of another more experienced person. The length of the practicum will vary with the individual but generally should be limited to three times.

4. Don't Overlook the Little Things

A trainer should never make an assumption about a high level of experience or knowledge in volunteers. Err on the side of giving details. It is much easier to speed up a training process than to increase the content once it has begun.

115

A secretary who is instructing a volunteer in typing ought to review the various parts of the machine as well as the kinds of supplies that are needed. It may seem unnecessary to the secretary to point out the on and off switch to an electric typewriter or how a person sets margins, but these are the little things that are too embarrassing to ask about. When the secretary includes them, the volunteer can learn without exposing a lack of experience on the machine used in the church office.

In training, as in most other things, it is the little items that are easily overlooked but which can cause the greatest frustration. These little things include how to use correction fluid when typing on a stencil or where to place the cards after using them in a visit, or where the key to the supply closet is kept. There are a hundred other things that have become automatic to an experienced person but are a mystery to a new volunteer. Volunteers must be fully informed about their jobs, especially the little things that affect their tasks.

Working schedules of the church staff is an important bit of information for volunteers. For example, if the office closes at 11:30 A.M. and remains closed until 1:00 P.M., this is important to know. If there is a change in hours according to the day of the week or if there are evening hours, the volunteers should be informed. This information must be repeated often. It ought not to be assumed that a volunteer will know or remember the times of staff availability.

Having said all this, I must still emphasize that each task will have its uniqueness. This is the beauty of working in the church. One can choose from among many alternatives in seeking to express mission. Thus, during that second hour of training and the subsequent practicum, each job should be dealt with individually. The training experiences will be tailored to the job. The little items will be taken care of before they become stumbling blocks of frustration.

116

5. Follow-up Training

Follow-up, on-the-job assistance may be used to compensate for individual differences in volunteers. This must be in the form of assistance in particular trouble spots. It should not become a time in which the pastor or church staff member personally takes over the job. In other words, it should not be the type of follow-up used by the minister who could not allow volunteers to contribute their skills to the church. It ought to be an enabling kind of effort. This means that the pastor or whoever is responsible must be sensitive to the abilities and personal motivations of the volunteer. Taking over a volunteer's task is easy, but that defeats the purpose of developing a style of church life encouraging participation. It limits the potential of the church to be a witnessing community.

Pictures and Experiences

Elsewhere I have written about the use of the overhead projector in the church (*Media: Library Services Journal.* Jan. Feb. Mar. 1979. Nashville, Southern Baptist Sunday School Board.), expressing my conviction that illustrations and pictures and practical experiences are the best ways to teach adults. If the two-hour training plan is followed, illustrations and pictures ought to be used liberally during the first hour. The second hour can be built around practical experiences, especially if this includes practice or role-plays.

It takes a little extra time to create illustrations, but simple lists on an overhead projector can do wonders. It will help both the trainer and trainee by presenting a visual as well as a spoken listing.

Films and film strips are good for background or generalized information in certain settings. These must not be used as substitutes for training. The best training involves a person speaking to other persons. The trainer may use a visual aid, but an aid cannot answer questions or

reexplain a task. Training is for preparation to work in a specific church in a specific task. Generalized treatment of a job is not complete enough. Films and filmstrips may be good introductions but cannot meet the needs of training in each church.

Nonstop lectures are not as good as training events. Effective training involves give and take between the trainer and the trainees. People need to have the opportunity to ask questions, to hear again the objectives and purposes and goals of the church, to probe the trainer on particular points. Even the most flamboyant lecturer in the world cannot train a group merely by holding them spellbound for an hour. It is far better to think of training as a time when practice and experience are stressed.

This is not to suggest that training sessions are dry, dull, and boring. The converse is the case. People are interested in doing a good job. It is not the purpose of a trainer to discourage them by doing a terrible or merely passable job of training. It should be interesting and informing. It must send the volunteers away from the session with the information they need to do an effective job. It ought to inspire and increase their motivation. Pictures and illustrations can help in all these objectives.

Sequence of Job Steps

An important discipline for a person recruiting and training volunteers is to write down for them exactly the steps needed to do a job. This can be done in a way that will permit the person to use his or her creativity. It is done as a sequencing of the steps needed for a job, a chart of activity. This can save volunteers considerable time in figuring out an approach to a task.

As a trainer is writing the steps down, the exercise may seem so elementary that he or she believes everyone already knows everything that is to be done. Do not be fooled. Even

119

the most experienced volunteer can learn new things when presented with another person's step-by-step outline.

Take the task of leading a meeting for example. A sequence of the jobs would look like this:

1. Write down the purpose.
2. Identify, enumerate, and record the goals that the meeting is to accomplish.
3. List the members of the committee and others who will be invited to attend.
4. Set the time and place for the meeting.
5. Contact the persons by deciding how or who will do the contacting, in what form, and if there is to be a response from the attendants.
6. Set the agenda. This will require some consultation with the pastor or church staff member and probably a member or two of the committee.
7. Finalize the agenda and note the items that can be postponed until later if necessary.
8. Contact those who will be making reports to be certain that they, or at least their reports, will be at the meeting.
9. Make certain that the church or place of meeting will be open and heated or cooled at least fifteen minutes prior to the meeting time.
10. Have in mind how this meeting may result in further action and have a proposal for how any such action might be pursued.

Developing such a step-by-step procedure for a meeting takes time and energy. A trainer will help the inexperienced chairperson learn how this is done, will stress that each step be listed and checked off as it is accomplished, and will identify the most important parts in the process. Those who have been chairpersons for some time have their own ways of preparing. They may feel that presenting a step-by-step procedure is too cumbersome and involved. No matter.

They should have the opportunity to go over the process of sequencing their preparation and activity. It may be discovered that some of them have been skipping certain things or not being thorough in their preparation. As they develop a more systematic approach to their jobs, their performance and that of the committee will undoubtedly improve.

Resources

A question in each volunteer's mind concerns resources. This need for information must be dealt with during the training session. "Resources" is an inclusive term. It includes information about people who can help with a task, what supplies are needed and where they are available, reimbursement for expenses that might be incurred, and the availability of the pastor or church staff for counsel or in cases of emergency.

Resources involve the mundane things of life and are therfore of vital importance to the volunteer. Four things about resources need to be highlighted.

1. Financial Resources

It takes some time in a training session, but providing information about *financial* resources will save time later on. For example, a young mother was creating and maintaining a library for her church. She was at the church at least one and sometimes two mornings a week. In addition, she was on the phone at home several times each week. She had two small children at home who were too young for school.

After about a year, during which the library was established and was being used, although somewhat sparingly, this woman told the pastor she could not continue. He was flabbergasted. "Did we do something wrong?"

"Oh no. I enjoy the library. It gets me out of the house and

121

makes me keep up with my reading. It is a rewarding experience."

"What is the matter that you feel you must resign?"

The woman was very hesitant but finally said, "I really cannot afford to continue. No one from my family lives near here, and I must pay for the baby-sitter each time I come. For a while I thought we could handle it ourselves, but we have been hit by some large, unexpected bills. It is impossible for us to continue to pay the four to five dollars it costs each time I come down to work for the church."

"Why didn't you say so? We have a fund that pays for baby-sitters for volunteers. In fact, sometimes baby-sitters are provided here at the church. You only need to ask."

Why must a volunteer be put in a position of asking? It is the responsibility of the church to let volunteers know about any resources that are available. In this instance, knowledge about baby-sitter reimbursement would have relieved this woman and her husband of the strain of making an unnecessary decision. This is the kind of information that should have been included in the training session. Unfortunately, that church did not train its volunteers so there was no opportunity to give this woman the message about this resource. The pastor felt training was too time-consuming for himself as well as for the volunteers.

2. Budgeting Procedures

Training includes helping volunteers handle budget and money items. This part of the training session ought to be done carefully. The fine details may be postponed until later when individual attention is given to each volunteer, but the general procedures used in the church need to be explained during the first session. This will include noting the amount of money available for any or all of the jobs, any need for cut-backs that may be coming, and who handles various types of accounts.

3. People-Resources

It is as important for a volunteer to know about people-resources as it is about finances. A list of individuals experienced in various jobs can be a helpful addition to the training experience. The person who has held the position or done the job in the recent past now assumed by another is an individual who could give some help to the new recruit. In every congregation, there are members who have done the jobs that other volunteers take on. These more experienced members can be a valuable resource to the new persons. Letting the trainees know about predecessors adds resources to their lists.

4. Resource Lists

One objective of the training session is to identify for the volunteer as many potential resources as possible. It is not expeced that a volunteer will make contact with or use all the resources. It is important that each volunteer has a list for reference so that in times of need, those lists might be used.

Creating resource lists can be relatively simple. For people-resources; the name, address, phone number, and the types of experiences are all that is necessary on a card. When the list concerns money; the various forms and requisitions needed, the types of reporting required, and information about who authorizes expenditures will suffice. In listing supplies, any forms that are to be used should be displayed and explained.

Flexibility

A final item included in a training session is the formula for flexibility used in the church. This includes giving volunteers the time schedule for the office, where to reach the pastor or staff members in the evenings or on weekends, and the way to arrange to work on "odd hour" schedules.

123

For example, a man may need to work between 4:30 and 6:00 P.M. on Wednesday as a volunteer typist. This is the most convenient time during the week for him. The church office, however, closes at 4:30 every day of the week. Does this mean he cannot be a volunteer? The answer in some churches is a surprising yes. The schedule is fixed, and volunteers must fit in with it or find something else or someplace else to give their time and energy. A reasonable congregation, however, will recognize that people have different availabilities and will work out the arrangements for encouraging flexible working hours.

A different type of flexibility is to take work to the volunteer. If this is an option in the church for certain types of work, the procedure for doing this ought to be spelled out in the training sessions. Whatever the policies or practices relating to timing and scheduling of work must be laid before the volunteers prior to their beginning their assignments.

The final part of the training process is to let the volunteers know how to go about changing their tasks or resigning. To present this to the volunteers in an open and straightforward manner is to relieve them of possible embarrassment when they feel they must resign.

Not everyone who agrees to a task is able to complete that job. The reasons are multiple. Rather than cause an individual to feel like a failure, it is much better to spell out in detail for everyone the procedure to follow should it become necessary to withdraw. When this is done as a normal part of the training, a person who withdraws can feel free to volunteer at a more opportune time or when another job more to his or her liking is available.

Conclusion

The objectives for training sessions are to inform volunteers of opportunities, of resources, of the operational style of the congregation, and of the procedures when withdrawal from an assignment is necessary. Another objective is to strengthen the motivation that leads people to work in the church. Inspiration is a major plus in any training event.

Preparation for training sessions should be taken seriously by the pastor, trainer, and church staff. Each must have a clear understanding of what is being expected from each volunteer. This ought to be accompanied with a careful inventory of the probable needs that person will have in the way of resources, money, and people during the job.

Training should not play down creativity and the need for the volunteer to approach a job in his or her own manner. This means that the training session will stress skills and procedures without dictating style. After all, each volunteer brings a uniqueness to the task that should be allowed to show through. Only in this way can the volunteer experience a feeling of having done something worthwhile for the church. This can become that individual's expression of ministry.